P9-CRF-795

THE HUMANS

BY
STEPHEN KARAM

★

★

DRAMATISTS
PLAY SERVICE
INC.

THE HUMANS
Copyright © 2016, Stephen Karam

All Rights Reserved

CAUTION: Professionals and amateurs are hereby warned that performance of THE HUMANS is subject to payment of a royalty. It is fully protected under the copyright laws of the United States of America, and of all countries covered by the International Copyright Union (including the Dominion of Canada and the rest of the British Commonwealth), and of all countries covered by the Pan-American Copyright Convention, the Universal Copyright Convention, the Berne Convention, and of all countries with which the United States has reciprocal copyright relations. All rights, including without limitation professional/amateur stage rights, motion picture, recitation, lecturing, public reading, radio broadcasting, television, video or sound recording, all other forms of mechanical, electronic and digital reproduction, transmission and distribution, such as CD, DVD, the Internet, private and file-sharing networks, information storage and retrieval systems, photocopying, and the rights of translation into foreign languages are strictly reserved. Particular emphasis is placed upon the matter of readings, permission for which must be secured from the Author's agent in writing.

The English language stock and amateur stage performance rights in the United States, its territories, possessions and Canada for THE HUMANS are controlled exclusively by DRAMATISTS PLAY SERVICE, INC., 440 Park Avenue South, New York, NY 10016. No professional or nonprofessional performance of the Play may be given without obtaining in advance the written permission of DRAMATISTS PLAY SERVICE, INC., and paying the requisite fee.

Inquiries concerning all other rights should be addressed to William Morris Endeavor Entertainment, LLC, 11 Madison Avenue, 18th floor, New York, NY 10010. Attn: John Buzzetti.

SPECIAL NOTE
Anyone receiving permission to produce THE HUMANS is required to give credit to the Author as sole and exclusive Author of the Play on the title page of all programs distributed in connection with performances of the Play and in all instances in which the title of the Play appears, including printed or digital materials for advertising, publicizing or otherwise exploiting the Play and/or a production thereof. Please see your production license for font size and typeface requirements.

Be advised that there may be additional credits required in all programs and promotional material. Such language will be listed under the "Additional Billing" section of production licenses. It is the licensee's responsibility to ensure any and all required billing is included in the requisite places, per the terms of the license.

THE HUMANS had its world premiere at American Theater Company (PJ Paparelli, Artistic Director), Chicago, Illinois, in November 2014. It was directed by PJ Paparelli, the set design was by Dave Ferguson, the costume design was by Brittany Dee Bodley, the lighting design was by Brian Hoehne, the sound design was by Patrick Bely, and the stage manager was Amanda Davis. The cast was as follows:

ERIK BLAKE .... Keith Kupferer
DEIRDRE BLAKE .... Hanna Dworkin
AIMEE BLAKE .... Sadieh Rifai
BRIGID BLAKE .... Kelly O'Sullivan
FIONA "MOMO" BLAKE .... Jean Moran
RICHARD SAAD .... Lance Baker

THE HUMANS was commissioned and originally produced Off-Broadway by Roundabout Theatre Company, at the Laura Pels Theatre, opening on October 25, 2015. It was directed by Joe Mantello, the scenic design was by David Zinn, the costume design was by Sarah Laux, the lighting design was by Justin Townsend, the sound design was by Fitz Patton, the production stage manager was William Joseph Barnes, and the stage manager was Devin Day. The cast was as follows:

ERIK BLAKE .... Reed Birney
DEIRDRE BLAKE .... Jayne Houdyshell
AIMEE BLAKE .... Cassie Beck
BRIGID BLAKE .... Sarah Steele
FIONA "MOMO" BLAKE .... Lauren Klein
RICHARD SAAD .... Arian Moayed

The Roundabout production of THE HUMANS transferred to the Helen Hayes Theatre on Broadway, with the same cast and creative team, on January 23, 2016. The Broadway production was produced by Scott Rudin, Barry Diller, Roundabout Theatre Company, Fox Theatricals, James L. Nederlander, Terry Allen Kramer, Roy Furman, Daryl Roth, Jon B. Platt, Eli Bush, Scott M. Delman, Sonia Friedman, Amanda Lipitz, Peter May, Stephanie P. McClelland, Lauren Stein and the Shubert Organization, and Joey Parnes (Sue Wagner and John Johnson, executive producers).

DRAMATIS PERSONAE

ERIK BLAKE, 60

DEIRDRE BLAKE, 61, Erik's wife

AIMEE BLAKE, 34, their daughter

BRIGID BLAKE, 26, their daughter

FIONA "MOMO" BLAKE, 79, Erik's mother

RICHARD SAAD, 38, Brigid's boyfriend

NOTES

1.) A slash (/) means the character with the next line of dialogue begins their speech.

2.) Dialogue in brackets [ ] is expressed non-verbally.

3.) *The Humans* takes place in one real-time scene—on a two-level set—with no blackouts. Life continues in all spaces at all times.

4.) *The Humans* explores the fears of a middle class family—not necessarily a white middle class family. Though the family's heritage draws from my own background (I am half Irish-American, half Lebanese-American), the primary obsession of the play isn't unpacking of the Irish-American experience; as such, I hope families of all ethnicities will be gathered around the table in future productions. The casting of actors of color shouldn't be viewed as a radical concept, nor one that requires the author's permission.

—SK

There are six basic fears, with some combination of which every human suffers at one time or another...

   The fear of POVERTY
   The fear of CRITICISM
   The fear of ILL HEALTH
   The fear of LOSS OF LOVE OF SOMEONE
   The fear of OLD AGE
   The fear of DEATH

—Napoleon Hill,
Think and Grow Rich

The subject of the "uncanny"... belongs to all that is terrible— to all that arouses dread and creeping horror... The German word [for "uncanny"], unheimlich, *is obviously the opposite of* heimlich, *meaning "familiar," "native," "belonging to the home"; and we are tempted to conclude that what is "uncanny" is frightening precisely because it is not known and familiar... [But] among its different shades of meaning the word* heimlich *exhibits one which is identical with its opposite,* unheimlich... *on the one hand, it means that which is familiar and congenial, and on the other, that which is concealed and kept out of sight.*

—Sigmund Freud,
"The Uncanny"

THE HUMANS

A turn-of-the-century ground floor/basement duplex tenement apartment in New York City's Chinatown. It's just big enough to not feel small. It's just small enough to not feel big.

The two floors are connected via a spiral staircase. Each floor has its own entrance.

The apartment's pre-war features have been coated in layers of faded off-white paint, rendering the space curiously monotone. The rooms are worn, the floors are warped, but clean and well kept.

The layout doesn't adhere to any sensible scheme—the result of a mid-century renovation in which two autonomous apartments were combined.

Upstairs*: two rooms divided by an open entryway. The room with the staircase also has the apartment's lone, large, deep-set window with bars. The window gets no direct sunlight. An urban recliner is the only piece of furniture upstairs. The other room has a door that leads to the duplex's sole bathroom.*

Downstairs*: two windowless rooms divided by an even larger open entryway—with a different floorplan than upstairs. A small kitchen alley is wedged awkwardly behind the spiral staircase. The other room is dominated by a modest folding table. The table is set with six paper plates and napkins with turkeys on them. Plastic silverware. Scattered moving boxes. Not much else.*

The apartment is a touch ghostly, but not in a forced manner; empty pre-war basement apartments are effortlessly uncanny.

At lights: Erik is upstairs, alone, some plastic bags in his hands. Beside him is an empty wheelchair. He takes in the space. The main door is open. Beat.

A sickening THUD sounds from above the ceiling. Erik looks up.

ERIK. [What the hell was that?]

> *He recovers.*
> *Gradually his attention shifts away from the noise; he continues to explore the space when—*
> *Another sickening THUD sounds from above, startling him.*
> *He looks up.*

[God, what the hell is that?]

> *A toilet flush.*
> *Aimee and Brigid enter through the main door carrying a few plastic bags.*

AIMEE. This is the last of the goodies...

BRIGID. *(To Erik.)* I told you guys not to bring anything.

> *Deirdre and Momo exit the bathroom; Momo is shaky on her feet. Erik helps her into her wheelchair.*

DEIRDRE. Mission accomplished...

BRIGID. It's pretty big, right?

AIMEE.	ERIK.
Definitely bigger than	I gotcha Mom,
your last place.	there you go...

ERIK. Is there some kinda construction going on upstairs?

BRIGID. Oh, no that's our neighbor, we think she drops stuff? Or stomps around?—we don't know...

> **Downstairs**: *Richard emerges from the kitchen alley.*

RICHARD. *(Calling up.)* Everyone okay up there?

BRIGID. We're fine, babe, just keep an eye on the oven, we'll be down in a minute.

RICHARD. You got it.

ERIK. Have you complained to her about the noise?

BRIGID. No, Dad, she's a seventy-year-old Chinese woman, / I'm not gonna—

DEIRDRE. Well, Brigid, I'm sixty-one—older people can still process information, we're / still able to—

BRIGID. I'm saying she means well, she's older so I don't wanna disturb her if I don't have to /... Hey, here, I'll take your coats...

MOMO. *(Mumbled.)* You can never come back... you can never come back /... you can never come back... cannevery you come back...

DEIRDRE. Alright... you're alright, Mom...

> *Momo's mumbling is not directed to anyone—her primary focus is down, towards the floor, lost; she is passive and disconnected.*

BRIGID. What's she saying?

DEIRDRE.	MOMO.
She's—[who the hell knows] —even when she *is* sayin' real stuff... what's been comin' out is still all... [muddled]	... fernall heres ullerin... werstrus um black... sezz it bigger... fernal down / black... sornit all...

ERIK. Mom, hey Mom, this is Brigid's new apartment...

BRIGID. How are you, Momo?

DEIRDRE. We're gonna have Thanksgiving at your granddaughter's new place, / that sound good?

MOMO. *(Mumbled.)* ... you can never come back... you can never come back...

BRIGID. Momo, you can absolutely come back, any time you want.

> *Deirdre moves into the room with the recliner.*

ERIK. This is a decent layout, Bridge... / good space...

11

DEIRDRE. Really nice…

BRIGID. It's good, right?—I can set up my music workspace downstairs so I won't drive Rich crazy.

DEIRDRE. This is a fancy chair… Erik, check out this fancy chair…

ERIK. I thought all your furniture was on the moving truck.

BRIGID. It is—Richard's parents gave us that—a couch, too… we're not sure if the living area'll be up here or—this might become the bedroom…

AIMEE. *(Noticing the staircase.)* I can't believe you have a downstairs…

ERIK. Why would they give something this nice away?

BRIGID.	MOMO. *(Softly mumbled.)*
Because they got a new one, Dad.	… fernall all sertrus inner…

DEIRDRE. *(Re: the recliner.)* You might want something even bigger up here…

BRIGID. This isn't Scranton, I don't need an oversized recliner in every room.

MOMO. *(Mumbled.)* … you can never come back… you can never come back…

Erik is drawn to the window, studies the surroundings.

BRIGID. Momo…?

DEIRDRE. It's her latest phrase-of-the-day… The doctor says it's normal, the repeating…

BRIGID. And… how's she been?

Eriks stops staring out the window.
Momo's face remains blank and focused on the floor.

ERIK. Uh… she's still got her good days, you know?… Yesterday

12

she was pretty with it for most of the morning, but now she's [all over the place]... I dunno where she goes...

DEIRDRE. I tried to do her hair, I want her to look good, / you know?

AIMEE.   BRIGID.
She does...   Treat yourself to a spa day...
                                    / the both of you should go—

DEIRDRE. No, no way, do you know how much that costs?

BRIGID. Yeah, well you'll burn out if you're / not careful—

DEIRDRE. Hey, hey don't worry about us—having her at home with us is, until it becomes too much, it's a blessing, you know... right Erik?... Erik...

> *Erik has been staring out the window—something outside caught his attention.*

AIMEE. *Dad— /* come back to earth...

ERIK. Sorry, sorry... long drive.

BRIGID. Are you okay?

ERIK. Yeah, once I get some caffeine in me, I'll be good...

AIMEE. *(Trying to find the light switch in the bathroom.)* Hey is the light switch...?

BRIGID. No, it's on the outside...

> *Another THUD sounds above the ceiling. Erik is the only one who looks up.*

ERIK. You want me to call the super about the noise?—

BRIGID. No, no this is New York, people are loud, why are you so—

DEIRDRE. Hey, he had a rough night, he hasn't been sleeping, /
he's been—Erik, you haven't...

ERIK.	BRIGID.
Deirdre, c'mon... [please	Why haven't you been sleeping?
don't talk about this...]	Are you okay?...
(To Brigid.) I'm—yeah,	
I'm okay...	

AIMEE. *(O.S., from behind the door.)* There's no toilet paper!

BRIGID. Okay, hang on...

> *Brigid searches for toilet paper in one of the boxes/shopping
> bags. Deirdre follows her.*

ERIK. Hey you get cell reception in here?

BRIGID. Up here we do, if—is it a Verizon phone?

ERIK. Uh, Sprint.

BRIGID. Then you have to lean up against the window.

ERIK. In here? I wanna check the score of the game.

BRIGID. Yeah... but now, yeah, now lean in...

> *Erik sits in the window ledge trying to get reception. Brigid
> looks for toilet paper.*

DEIRDRE. The sheets were covered in sweat last night... I dunno
if he's havin' nightmares or what—

BRIGID. Rich sometimes takes a sleeping pill, I can ask him what
kind of / medicine—

DEIRDRE. Oh right like your dad'd ever try any sorta—no, no
I bet... he'll sleep better after seein' you guys today, it'll be good
for him...

BRIGID. Okay... well, good...

Brigid cracks the bathroom door open, hands Aimee the toilet paper, then shuts the door.

DEIRDRE. ... Yeah...

AIMEE. *(O.S.)* Thank you.

BRIGID. ... And... how's Aimee?...

DEIRDRE. [I dunno]... she's still heartbroken, you know?...

BRIGID. [Yeah,] it's gonna be weird for *us*, not having Carol around...

DEIRDRE. Well I'm telling you if they got married it—

BRIGID.	DEIRDRE.
Mom...	—hey, it's why I don't like you and Rich moving in together before
I know, Mom but—	making a real commitment—

DEIRDRE. —marriage can help you weather a storm, / that's all—

BRIGID. —okay, but we put this to rest, / yeah?...

DEIRDRE. I know, yeah, I'm sorry.

MOMO. Sorn it allinners, / sorn it all...

BRIGID. *(Noticing Momo's runny nose.)* Mom—Momo's nose...

DEIRDRE. Oh God... *(Lovingly wiping Momo's nose.)* ... There we go, Mom, there we go...

ERIK. The Lions are up seven.

DEIRDRE.	BRIGID.
Thank God, we can eat in peace.	Yay...

BRIGID. Sorry you're not sleeping, Big Guy...

ERIK. I'm fine.

BRIGID. … Do you want to put your feet up and take a quick nap before dinner?—

ERIK. *(Amused by her worry.)* No way, are you kidding me?, / no…

BRIGID. I'm serious!

ERIK. … No, I'm good…

BRIGID. Rich hasn't been sleeping much either, he's been having weird dreams about—he thinks they're related to the stress of the move…

DEIRDRE. Oh man…

BRIGID. … Yeah, and he's been keeping *me* up while he tries to unravel their meaning.

DEIRDRE. Why's he doing that?

BRIGID. He took *one* psychology course last year and suddenly he's an armchair psychiatrist.

RICHARD. *(Calling up.)* I took *two* psychology courses!

BRIGID. [One.]	DEIRDRE. *(Calling down.)* Hey there, Rich!…
RICHARD. *(Calling up.)* Hey, I'll be up in a minute!…	ERIK. Bridge—hey… I keep noticin' a lotta—you guys gotta caulk all along the molding down there… / there's big gaps there…

BRIGID. Thanks, okay Repairman, thank you, but can you at least… someone needs to say something about my big window. No one has said anything about my big window…

16

DEIRDRE. *(Aside, to Erik.)* I love seeing her this excited, don't you love seeing her / this excited?

ERIK. Yeah, I do, we don't have to talk about it.

> *Brigid walks into the area near the spiral staircase, searches for something amidst the boxes.*

RICHARD. *(Calling up.)* Honey bring down the napkins, okay?

BRIGID. Richard, what are you yelling at me?

RICHARD. I said: bring down the napkins please!	***Upstairs:*** *Unseen by Brigid, Deirdre* *and Erik confer about some-* *thing in the hallway or next* *room. They are audible-but-* *not-decipherable.*
BRIGID. Yeah, Richard, or you can get them yourself.	
	The tail end of their conversation:
RICHARD. Do you / want me to—	DEIRDRE. Okay, but /… if you wait—
BRIGID. *(Meeting him halfway down the stairs.)* No I got them, sorry…	ERIK. Hey—gimme some space, I will… I will—
	DEIRDRE. Okay, I just don't want—

> ***Upstairs:*** *Brigid hears the tail end of Deirdre's private discussion with Erik. Aimee exits the bathroom.*

BRIGID. You guys better not be dissing my home—do you even get how special a place like this is? No New Yorkers have duplex apartments.

AIMEE. Except for the thousands of New Yorkers who have duplex apartments—

BRIGID. I *knew* you were gonna / say that—

AIMEE. Oh come on, I love it… / it's amazing…

ERIK.   DEIRDRE.
We all love it…   Me too, but… why are there bars
                                        on the window? Is the neighbor-
                                        hood dangerous?

AIMEE. *(Smiling.)*   BRIGID.
Mom, no…   No that's standard for a ground-
                                        floor apartment—

BRIGID. … after a while you don't even notice them—

DEIRDRE. Yeah, you don't notice them 'cause there's no sunlight
in here… / it's like a cave…

BRIGID. Mom…

ERIK. *(Looking out the window.)* Hey, who's walkin' around out there?

BRIGID. Uh, must be the super, he's the only one who has access.

ERIK. No, she's got gray hair?

BRIGID. *(Looking outside.)* Lemme see… where?

        Erik looks back out the window; this time he sees nothing.

ERIK. She went inside, I guess…

        Brigid moves away from the window.

BRIGID. Probably the super's wife, I haven't met her yet. *(To Erik, who
is still staring out the window.)* Hey, Detective… sit down and relax.

DEIRDRE. I wish you had more of a view—

BRIGID. Mom…

DEIRDRE. What?—it's an alley full of cigarette butts—

BRIGID. It's an *interior courtyard*… / not a—

18

ERIK.
Oh, excuse me...

DEIRDRE. *(Looking out the window.)*
Well hey now, Fancy... perhaps we should all take a stroll in the interior courtyard after dinner.

Brigid sighs, she knows she can't win.

BRIGID. Okay, yes, it's gross, smokers use the alley as their ashtray, but... you don't think this place has potential?

ERIK. I think if you moved to Pennsylvania your quality of life would shoot up.

BRIGID. Uh, if I moved to Pennsylvania, *your* quality of life would shoot up / tremendously—

DEIRDRE.
Don't flatter yourself, lady—

ERIK.
Oh yeah?

ERIK. What makes you think we like you so much?

BRIGID. You drove in from Scranton in the snow.

ERIK. The roads are all plowed.

Brigid hugs him. Deirdre recognizes a box.

DEIRDRE. Is this our—Bridge, you didn't even *open* our care package?

BRIGID. I'm not opening *anything* until the moving truck gets here—

ERIK. Is it in transit or / is it still—

BRIGID. No, no it's still stuck in Queens—Rich knows the details, but—now with the parade traffic, they won't guarantee their mechanic'll fix it before tomorrow...

Brigid finds what she has been looking for: a bag with several wrapped objects.

19

DEIRDRE. What's all that?

BRIGID. *(Handing out the wrapped packages.)* You guys went out of your way to get here, / so… open…

DEIRDRE. What is it?…

BRIGID. Open, open…

AIMEE. What did you get us?	DEIRDRE. Thank you… Erik don't [throw your wrapping away]—I wanna save the wrapping…

They each unwrap a framed photo.

ERIK. Oh man…

AIMEE. You gotta be kidding me…	DEIRDRE. Oh God…

Aimee laughs.

ERIK. Wow…

BRIGID. Found it when I was packing.

DEIRDRE. … Oh man… were we ever this young?… Look how *young* you are, Aimee…

AIMEE. I'm an elephant in this photo…

DEIRDRE. You're beautiful.	BRIGID. No…

AIMEE. … And I'm holding a funnel cake… I can't even blame genetics…

ERIK. This is gold, Brigid, / thanks. Check it out, Mom…

DEIRDRE. It really is, honey… thank you.

AIMEE. I am a *planet* in this photo.

ERIK.   DEIRDRE.
You look beautiful.   Stop it, I'm bigger than you...

DEIRDRE. I miss Wildwood...

BRIGID.   ERIK.
Go back, take a vacation...   Oh man, that boardwalk...

DEIRDRE. Talk to this one, he hates traveling—

ERIK. I do not / hate traveling—

BRIGID. You hate traveling to New York—

ERIK. I do not hate traveling to New / York, no, no, I don't...

DEIRDRE.   AIMEE.
Yes you do!   Okay, that's a lie.

ERIK. ... I *hate* that you moved a few blocks from where two towers
got blown up and in a major flood zone... / I hate *that*...

BRIGID. This area is safe—

ERIK. Chinatown *flooded* during the last hurricane— / it flooded—

BRIGID. Yeah, that's why I can afford to live here—it's not like
you gave me any money to help me out.

ERIK.   BRIGID.
Wow...   Hey, I'm—sorry, just... Chinatown
                                   is safe /—you saw my block, Dad—

DEIRDRE. Of course it is...

BRIGID. —No one's gonna steer a plane into a, a fish market on
Grand Street—

21

AIMEE.	DEIRDRE.
Brigid...	Let it go...

ERIK. I liked you livin' in Queens, alright? I worry enough with Aimee on the top floor of the Cira Centre—

AIMEE. Well stop, Philly is more stable than New York—

BRIGID. Aimee, don't / make him more—

AIMEE. I'm just saying—it's safer...

BRIGID. Yeah, 'cause not even terrorists wanna spend time in Philly, / Philly is awful—

AIMEE. Oh, ha ha...

ERIK. You think everything's awful, you think *Scranton* is awful, / but it's the place that—

BRIGID.	AIMEE.
We *think* it's awful?!	Dad, it is!

ERIK. *(Their amusement forces him to smile.)* ... yeah, well what *I* think's funny is how you guys, you move to big cities and trash Scranton, when Momo almost killed herself gettin' outta New York—she didn't have a real toilet in this city, and now her grand-daughter moves right back to the place / she struggled to escape...

BRIGID. We know, yes... "return to the slums"...

DEIRDRE. It's not the slums anymore...

ERIK. Oh man, that store—on the corner of Eldridge?—we went in to get you a candle—

DEIRDRE. Don't *tell* her that, we didn't end up buying it—

ERIK. The most expensive candles I've ever seen in my life.

AIMEE. *(A gentle reality check.)* They were twenty-five dollars.

ERIK.   DEIRDRE.
That's a lot of money!   For a *candle*?! That's insane, you
                                       should get five candles for that…

  Richard ascends the staircase with a bottle of champagne and
  plastic cups.

RICHARD. Hey, thought we could have a champagne toast up here?
Brigid claims we need to bless the upstairs *and* downstairs…

DEIRDRE.   BRIGID.
That is good Irish tradition, yessir… Yes, thanks, babe.

AIMEE. Should we sing Momo's favorite /—we have to, right?…

BRIGID. Of course we're gonna sing it! Rich has been warned.

  Under the following dialogue, Erik wanders into the adjoining
  room to grab a private moment for himself; he rubs his aching
  lower back, takes a deep breath.
  In the other room, Rich pours champagne into the plastic cups.

RICHARD. We only have plastic cups, but the good news is the
bar is set very low if we ever host again.

AIMEE.   DEIRDRE.
We could care less…   Thank you, Richard… cham-
                                       pagne'll make the cups feel
                                       fancy.

BRIGID. *(Calling into the other room.)* Dad…?

AIMEE. Did he sleep at *all* last night?

BRIGID.   DEIRDRE.
Yeah he seems—   I'm not gonna worry about
                                       him, okay, otherwise / I'll
                                       stop sleeping myself…

AIMEE. Okay, okay…

BRIGID. Alright, let's just, let's show Rich how badly our voices blend, / we'll do the money verses, yeah…?

AIMEE. Yeah, and FYI, I've been staying on key lately, you need to calm down…	RICHARD. I'm excited to hear this…

BRIGID. *You* need to calm down…	DEIRDRE. The Blakes have been singin' it for generations.

AIMEE. Will Momo join in if we—

DEIRDRE. Oh yeah—she's still good with music, Rich, wait'll you hear, / she'll join in…

BRIGID. *(Calling to the other room.)* —Dad! We're waiting for you… *(To Aimee.)* You want to start us off?…

AIMEE. No, no… I always start too high and you yell at me.

> *Erik enters the main room and starts to sing.*

ERIK.
> *Oh all / the money that e'er I had—*

Erik's singing elicits groans from the women.	BRIGID. Oh my God…

BRIGID. Get in here! That is a terrible key for me. Okay, Momes…

> *Erik joins the group in the next room. Brigid takes Momo's hand, sings to her.*

(Restarting in a better key for herself:)
> *Oh all the money that e'er I had,*
> *I lost it in good company*
Ladies… [join me…]

> *They look to Momo affectionately, expecting her to join in.*

24

BRIGID, AIMEE, and DEIRDRE.
And of all the harm that e'er I've done
Alas was done to none but me
And all I've done for want of wit
To memory now I can't recall

BRIGID. [Dad, you sing too...]

BRIGID, AIMEE, DEIRDRE, and ERIK.
Lay down your fears and raise your glass
May peace and joy be with you all

Momo remains blank.

DEIRDRE.	ERIK.
Aimee, take a verse...	... Yeah, you go Aimee...

AIMEE.
Oh may all the friends that e'er I had
They'd be sorry at my going away
I'm a lawyer, Rich—
(Back to singing.)
And may all the sweethearts that ere I had...
[Guys, sing with me please...]

BRIGID, AIMEE, and DEIRDRE.
They would wish me one more day to stay

Erik, sensing Aimee's sadness, takes over.

ERIK.
And if I had money enough to spend
and leisure time to sit awhile
(Indicating Deirdre:)
There is a maiden in this town
who sorely has my heart beguiled

DEIRDRE. Yeah, it better be me.

ERIK and BRIGID.
Her pale white cheeks her skin of snow,
I will not rest 'til she comes to call

BRIGID. Take it home…

BRIGID, AIMEE, DEIRDRE, and ERIK.
Lay down your fears and raise your glass
May peace and joy be with you all

> *They ad lib cheers, drink. The joy of the song is cut short by*
> *Momo's steady mumbling.*

MOMO. … nairywheres do we blag werstrus, doll sezzer / big sussten back… sezz it whairidoll… er hairin sildern fernal garn ackening ery or loddinsezz… *(Tapering to quiet under the family's conversation.)* … nairywheres do we blag werstrus, doll sezzer big sussten back… sezz it whairidoll… er hairin sildern fernal garn ackening ery or loddinsezz…

ERIK. *(Staying positive, massaging Momo's hand.)* Shhhh, alright… you're alright…

BRIGID. She normally joins in. This is new, / this is—

ERIK. Well it's—yeah, it's not one of her good days.

> *Small beat.*

DEIRDRE. I've missed hearing you sing, Bridge…

BRIGID. Mom, that's not even my strength…	DEIRDRE. … I'm serious, you sound good—

ERIK. You have any gigs lined up? Can we come embarrass you?—	RICHARD. *(To Deirdre.)* I agree.

BRIGID. No, I'm spending most of my nights bartending—you guys don't even know how much student debt I'm stuck with—

ERIK. Yeah, well, I *do* know who refused to go to a state school.

DEIRDRE. Ohhh, score one for Dad!	BRIGID. I knew you were gonna say that…

RICHARD. Why don't we—appetizers are out, / so just come down whenever you're ready…

BRIGID. Yes, good idea—let's move the party downstairs—

> *Everyone gathers their things, starts to move. Another THUD from above. Erik looks up; everyone else keeps moving. Brigid notices this.*

RICHARD. *(Halfway down the stairs.)* Sorry about the noise, guys…

BRIGID. *(To Erik.)* Hey… it's quieter down there… come down and unwind.

> *Brigid heads towards the stairwell. Richard arrives downstairs. Deirdre heads for the bathroom. Erik is still preoccupied with the noise, looking up.*
> *Brigid stops, she notices Erik isn't behind her. She turns and sees him staring at the ceiling.*

Dad, what're you doing?—go downstairs and relax, / please—

ERIK.	DEIRDRE.
Alright, okay…	I am, just gonna use the little girls' room first…

AIMEE. How do I get Momo down there…?

BRIGID. What do you mean?

AIMEE. Well I can't dump her down the spiral staircase.

BRIGID. Oh God, sorry, use the elevator—

ERIK. Here, I'll take her—

AIMEE. *(Taking control of the wheelchair.)* I got it, I never get to see her… go help Rich…

ERIK. You sure?

AIMEE. Yeah…

> *Erik heads downstairs. Brigid opens the door for Aimee and Momo.*

BRIGID. Take the elevator to the B level.

> **Downstairs:** *Erik descends the spiral staircase. Richard is making last-minute dinner preparations.*

(Calling down.) Rich, unlock the downstairs door please!

RICHARD. *(Calling up.)* You got it!

ERIK. Look at all this…

RICHARD. Come on down…

> **Upstairs:**

DEIRDRE. So when Momo needs the bathroom we've gotta go out in the hall and take the elevator?

BRIGID. Yeah, but… *I'll* take her back up if…

> *Deirdre sighs.*

Sorry, I forgot about her wheelchair.

DEIRDRE. Yeah, I know you did.

> **Upstairs:** *Deirdre enters the bathroom. Brigid heads for the staircase.*

> **Downstairs:** *Erik looks around, investigating.*

RICHARD. *(Handing Erik a beer.)* Beer?

ERIK. Yeah, I'll take a Coke, too, if you've got / soda or…

RICHARD. Yeah, coming right up…

ERIK. Thanks. Detroit's up seven.

RICHARD. Oh… oh, the football game?

Erik nods.

How's the lake house coming along? I hear you might build this summer?

ERIK. Uh, no, not until the sewers get put in… doesn't make sense to build with a septic system if they're gonna be putting in sewers soon.

BRIGID. *(Coming down the stairs.)* The sooner the better, I can't wait for a lake house Christmas.

RICHARD. *(Handing her a glass of wine.)* Red, right?

BRIGID. Yes, thank you… *(Re: the paper plates.)* … How do you like our fine china, Dad?

Erik smiles. Richard sets things out on the table, Brigid assists.

ERIK. You're gonna miss the old house.

BRIGID. I will; I won't miss the wall-to-wall carpeting… or the bunk beds.

Small beat. Erik drinks. Richard and Brigid prepare food in the kitchen alley.

RICHARD. Work's good, Erik?—you're still at—it's a Catholic high school, right?

BRIGID. St. Paul's, for twenty-eight years…

RICHARD. Wow, / that's impressive…

ERIK. Well…

BRIGID. They created a whole position for him.

ERIK. Don't make it sound—I headed up maintenance and coupla years ago they needed a, an Equipment Manager, so—

BRIGID. It's a big job, it's a triple-A school, he handles all the phys-ed classes, / manages the weight room, the kids love him...

ERIK. Alright, okay... hey enough...

RICHARD. That's impressive.

ERIK. It's practical. Got the girls free tuition. You don't pick up after other people's kids for twenty-eight years unless you really love your own, you know?

RICHARD. *(Toasting.)* Well, hey, to twenty-eight years...

BRIGID.	ERIK.
Twenty-eight years...	Cheers.

> **Upstairs**: *Toilet flush.*

> **Downstairs**: *Brigid—who was waiting for the bathroom to be free—starts up the staircase.*

RICHARD. Yeah, no it's crazy, our generation, we're lucky if we stay in a job for *one* year, right Bridge?

ERIK. Are you guys even *in* the same generation?

BRIGID. Dad, that's / not funny—

ERIK. What, I'm not allowed to joke?

BRIGID. No.

> **Upstairs**: *Deirdre exits the bathroom.*

> **Downstairs**: *Richard continues meal preparations.*

RICHARD. You decide on an architect for the lake house?

ERIK. Uh, no, that's a ways away.

> **Downstairs**: *Erik drinks.*

> **Upstairs**: *Brigid arrives, seeing Deirdre.*

BRIGID. Hey…

DEIRDRE. Your bathroom doesn't have a window…

BRIGID.	DEIRDRE.
I know, go downstairs.	… I love you, I'm just saying.

> *Upstairs: Brigid enters the bathroom. Deirdre goes into the other upstairs room to get her purse. She pulls out two wrapped presents. She moisturizes her hands. At some point on her way back to the stairs, she stops to eavesdrop on Richard and Erik's conversation.*

> *Downstairs:*

RICHARD. I actually like having the design process to look forward to, I like the planning stages.

ERIK. Yeah, well our budget's—we're gonna use one of those places where they've got pre-designed homes you can choose from? /… but…

RICHARD. Sure, good idea…

ERIK. … Yeah, and the place we're looking at has *good* designs, you know?…

RICHARD. Yeah, no that's great.

> *Richard prepares for dinner during the following exchange. He's listening, but multi-tasking.*

ERIK. I'll tell you, Rich, save your money now… I thought I'd be settled by my age, you know, but man, it never ends… mortgage, car payments, internet, our dishwasher just gave out…

RICHARD. Oh man…

ERIK. Yeah, yeah…

> *Small beat.*

… Dontcha think it should cost less to be alive?

RICHARD. Ha, absolutely…

ERIK. I even started cutting my own hair to try and save a few bucks… messed it up pretty good. Thank God I'm married.

Richard smiles. Erik drinks. Beat.

RICHARD.
So you want—no, sorry what?

ERIK.
Brigid said you're—

ERIK. [Nothing, nevermind.]

Erik drinks.

RICHARD. You want some ice?

ERIK. Uh, sure.

RICHARD. *(Getting the ice.)* So you've been… having some weird dreams too?

ERIK. Huh?

RICHARD. … Just… you can hear a lot through the [hole where the spiral staircase is], just caught that you haven't been sleeping, thought maybe—I've been having weird dreams all week, think it's because of the move… Last night I was polishing a silver refrigerator and… my dog was caught inside it?… and I don't have a dog? /… Just weird stuff…

ERIK. Oh man… sounds like it… No, I don't remember my [dreams]… even when I have one of those ones where, uh…

Erik takes a sip of beer.

RICHARD. What?

ERIK. … [No, nothing important…] You know the ones where you need a minute just to… figure out it isn't / actually [real]…

RICHARD. Oh, sure—

Knocking at the downstairs door startles Erik a bit—he spills his beer. Richard moves to help—

ERIK.
Sorry about that, Rich,
I got it, I got it...

RICHARD.
Don't worry about it—

More knocking. Richard opens the door as Erik cleans up his spill. Aimee wheels Momo inside.

RICHARD. Welcome... / come on in...

AIMEE. Hello, hello... so this is what lies beneath...

RICHARD. What are you drinking, Aimee?

AIMEE.
Whatever's open... red wine?
This is really a lot of space...

MOMO. *(Barely audible.)*
... where do we go... where
do we go...

RICHARD. Yeah if you sacrifice sunlight you can get some / extra square feet...

MOMO. *(Softly, mumbled.)* Where do we go? Where, where do we go? / Where do we go? Where do we go where do we go where do we go where do we go...

ERIK. Hey, you waking up a bit, Mom?...

AIMEE. She keeps asking me that—Momo we're going into this room is where we're going...

Upstairs: *Brigid exits the bathroom, is surprised to find Deirdre still upstairs.*

BRIGID. What are you doing?...

DEIRDRE.
Just wanted a breather...

Downstairs:
MOMO. *(Tapering to barely audible.)*
... where do we go do we go where
do we go do we go...

Downstairs: *Erik massages Momo's hand.*

33

Upstairs:

BRIGID. You're holding a present.

DEIRDRE. Ha, I am, it's for you and Rich. Open it downstairs…

BRIGID. Is it… a fancy candle?

DEIRDRE. Yeah, smart-ass, I'll give you a fancy candle… keep walking…

Upstairs: Deirdre and Brigid head downstairs.

Downstairs: Aimee unwinds with a glass of wine.

RICHARD. How's the law firm, Aimee?

AIMEE. Busy. M&A transactions are not a source of joy in my life, so—I'm glad you don't get cell reception down here, my Black-Berry needs the rest.

ERIK. She's an all-star there…

AIMEE. Dad, ugh, no—I was informed last month I'm no longer on the partner track, which—

DEIRDRE. *(Descending the staircase.)* What? / When did this—

ERIK. Does that mean it just takes more time? Or—

AIMEE. No, it's the nice way of saying: start looking for another job.

DEIRDRE.	ERIK.
Why would they / do that?—	Really?

AIMEE. It's complicated, / who knows…

BRIGID. I'm sorry.

AIMEE. … Yeah, I missed a lot of time last year when I was sick… / and then…

34

DEIRDRE. She's got ulcerative colitis, Rich—

AIMEE. ... Mom, okay—

DEIRDRE. —it affects the colon—

AIMEE. ... Okay, Mom, so... and I missed even *more* time right before they made their decision, I had another flare-up this month, so—

DEIRDRE.   ERIK.
Why didn't you tell us?   Oh babe, I'm sorry...

AIMEE. Because I don't want you to worry—

DEIRDRE. I would've sent you a care package...

AIMEE. Yeah, and a bunch of text messages asking about my bowel movements.

DEIRDRE. I just wanna know what's / going on.

ERIK.   AIMEE.
You know we'd do anything   I know, I know... I know,
for you, right?—   I do...

DEIRDRE. They can't fire you because of a medical condition—

AIMEE. Well they gave other reasons, obviously, but... yeah, you get the sense they support your chronic illness as long as it doesn't affect your billable hours.

BRIGID.   DEIRDRE.
I'm really sorry.   Well, they don't deserve you.

ERIK. How about... financially, are you okay, or—?

AIMEE. Yeah, I'm set for a while.

ERIK. For a few months, or—

AIMEE. Yeah, I'll let you know if I need money, I don't want to talk about my job or my— / let's talk about—

DEIRDRE. But just—how are you feeling?

AIMEE. Just minor cramping, I'm good, I am...

RICHARD. How about food-wise, can we get you / something special—

AIMEE. No, I'm fine, at ease, everyone, / really... let's...

BRIGID. *(Taking the spotlight off Aimee.)* Hey we should—why don't we do a downstairs toast, / before we forget, yeah?...

DEIRDRE. I'm okay with that...	AIMEE. Yes, / please...

BRIGID. Dad, will you lead us?...

RICHARD. I like this, being twice blessed...	ERIK. Sure, sure, how about...

ERIK. ... to the Blake family Thanksgiving...

DEIRDRE. ... to the very special Chinatown edition / of the Blake family Thanksgiving...

BRIGID. Yes, yes, yes...	AIMEE. Hear hear...

ERIK. Neither rain nor hail—	MOMO. Sorn it all...

DEIRDRE. Nor sleet nor snow... nor... what else?	... can neverbody black werstrus—

AIMEE. Nor ulcerative colitis...

MOMO. *(Mumbled.)* … can neverbody black werstrus—

BRIGID. Nor dementia…

MOMO. —you / sornum never back…

DEIRDRE.	AIMEE.
Okay, now you're pushing it…	Brigid…

BRIGID. *(Smiling.)* What—too soon? / Too soon?

AIMEE.	DEIRDRE.
Yes, too soon…	Not funny…

> *Brigid hugs Momo.*

ERIK. Yeah, you *better* give her a hug…

BRIGID. We love you Momes…

ERIK. To knowing this is what matters, right here… 'cause lemme tell you, coming down these streets, thinking about how far the Blakes've come… even seeing that candle store / was…

BRIGID. It's not a candle store, it's a boutique that sells, like, *one* candle—

ERIK. … Hey I'm just appreciating how, you see all these rich people walking around New York, God knows where their money comes from, but… end of the day, everything that *anyone's* got… I don't care how many candles you have… one day it *goes*… whatever gifts God's given us, in the end, no matter who you are… everything you have *goes*.

> *Small beat.*

DEIRDRE. Well that's the *positive* way of looking at things.

> *Erik smiles.*

ERIK. Sorry—I love my family… / that's the short version, I'm glad we're together.

AIMEE.
We love you too…

BRIGID.
Love you guys…

DEIRDRE.
Hear hear, Amen…

RICHARD.
Cheers…

ERIK. And a special thanks to Richard for making this meal possible, since we know what a lousy cook Brigid is…

BRIGID.
This is true…

AIMEE.
Amen.

They all ad lib cheers and toast.

RICHARD. Okay, five minutes and everything will be out and ready to go… *(Setting out more food.)* Here's some more munchies, here…

DEIRDRE. Yum… thank you…

They all settle in. Erik looks after Momo.

AIMEE. So how are you, Mom?

DEIRDRE. I'm good, I'm good… I was—did you get the text I sent about—Bridge, this girl who played basketball for Dunmore, she was bullied for being gay… her mom found her dead in her room on Tuesday…

BRIGID.
Whoa…

AIMEE.
Oh man…

DEIRDRE. … Yeah, suicide with some kinda pills… it's all over the news… I texted you, / I wasn't sure if you got it?

AIMEE. This week was crazy… no, yeah I got it, I'm just behind with my messages…

Deirdre picks at the crudité platter.

BRIGID. You don't have to text her every time a lesbian kills herself.

AIMEE.
She doesn't do that—I appreciate
what / you're meaning...

DEIRDRE.
I don't.

DEIRDRE. I get enough annoying forwards myself, so—I don't wanna clog up your guys's inbox—

AIMEE. You're not, Mom. You're good though?

DEIRDRE. I am, yeah... My bosses are—I'm an office manager, Rich, I've been with the same company since right outta high school...

ERIK. Whole place would fall apart without her—

DEIRDRE. ... Yeah, well my *salary* doesn't reflect that, and these new kids they hired, I'm working for two more guys in their twenties, and just 'cause they have a special degree they're making five times what I make, over forty years / I've been there, Rich...

RICHARD.
Wow, forty years...?

BRIGID.
Well... hey... focus on the lake house, you'll be able to unwind soon... you gotta take care of yourself.

AIMEE. Are you breaking ground this summer?

DEIRDRE. No...

RICHARD. It's smart to wait for the sewers, the value of your property will skyrocket.

AIMEE.
When are they gonna be installed?

BRIGID.
Thanks, Professor.

DEIRDRE. [I don't know...] Erik...?

ERIK. That's up to the department of public works, when the sewers get put in.

39

Small beat.

AIMEE. And how's Aunt Mary?

DEIRDRE. She's hanging in there, God love her… they got this contraption now to help load her into the pool but—Rich, this is their aunt who had both knees replaced, / I drive her to her physical therapy…

ERIK. *(Indicating the crudité platter.)* Pass the…

DEIRDRE. … And did I email you that—Kay Hoban has ovarian cancer…

AIMEE.	BRIGID.
Oh man… how's she doing?	She does? Yikes…

DEIRDRE. Yeah, I've been taking her to her treatments 'cause her and her brother, they don't speak anymore, so… that's a whole mess, but… she's being tough, so…

    Deirdre takes a bite of food.

… what else… oh, Tuesdays I'm now—

BRIGID. Mom, you're talking with your mouth full.

    Beat.

DEIRDRE. … I, uh, started volunteering for—Father Quinn told me about, and don't roll your eyes, Erik…

ERIK. I'm not saying a word.

DEIRDRE. … right in Scranton there's a whole community of refugees from Bhutan…

    Aimee stifles laughter.

What? / It's not funny…

BRIGID. Let me guess, Saint Deirdre is coming to their rescue?—

ERIK. *(Smiling.)* You have / no idea...

DEIRDRE. Be quiet—*you* have no idea—these people have *nothing*... they're all just looking to learn English, to find work—we *think* we've got nothing, but man...

RICHARD. That's great you're volunteering...

DEIRDRE. Thanks, Rich.

BRIGID. And how are *you*, Mom. Aimee didn't ask how the Republic of Bhutan was doing—

ERIK.   DEIRDRE.
Hey, hey...   I'm *good*, smart-ass, I said that
                                          already... Now why don't you
                                          open your gift...

BRIGID. Mom, I was just / teasing...

AIMEE. *(Getting up, registering a cramp.)* Hey guys—no one be alarmed if I'm up and down these stairs a million times to use the... facilities... so...

DEIRDRE. You want me to go with you?

> *Aimee shakes her head no as she goes up the stairs. Brigid opens her gift; it's a small, shiny pink pig.*

BRIGID. ... Ah, it's a peppermint pig! Rich, check it out...

DEIRDRE.   AIMEE.
Hey, holler if we can do anything, okay?   Amazing...

AIMEE. *(Going up the stairs.)* I will, don't smash that pig without me...

ERIK. We won't...

DEIRDRE. Poor baby...

BRIGID. And what is this other… *(Opening the other wrapped object.)* … Ah, a Virgin Mary statue—

DEIRDRE.
Okay, before you tease me I know you guys don't believe, but she's appearing everywhere now, not just in Fatima but in West Virginia and—just keep it for my sake, in the kitchen or even if you just put it in a drawer somewhere, okay?

BRIGID.
—complete with a serpent under her foot…

BRIGID. Mom, I will absolutely put this in a drawer somewhere, / thank you.

DEIRDRE. Yeah, well… I feel better knowing you have it.

RICHARD. I thought maybe Brigid was making the pig-smash up, but—

ERIK. Oh no, it's real…

RICHARD.
Can't wait to see how it works…

BRIGID.
It's not Thanksgiving without it… *(Hugging Deirdre.)* Thank you.

DEIRDRE. You're welcome.

MOMO. *(Quietly, tapering to silence.)* … why'm I hereson. Go warson herror truh. / Do the glassor comes blag… sezzor black… why'm I hereson. Go warson herror truh. Do the glassor comes blag… sezzor black… why'm I hereson. Go warson herror truh. Do the glassor comes blag… sezzor black…

DEIRDRE. *(Massaging Momo's hand.)* Okay, okay, you wanna go for a ride, Mom? Let's go for a ride…

> **Upstairs**: *Aimee nurses a cramp before she proceeds to the bathroom.*

Downstairs*: Deirdre wheels Momo around the apartment.*

ERIK. *(To Brigid and Rich, re: Momo.)* She had a good day yesterday, you know? It's hard to predict now how she's gonna be… This is definitely her last big trip…

BRIGID. How are *you* doing? Is that why you aren't you sleeping?—

ERIK.	RICHARD.
I'll sleep tonight—	Oh yeah, sorry Erik, we got sidetracked before—you were talking about your dream?

DEIRDRE. Oh, so you'll tell *him* details / about your dream—but you won't tell me?

RICHARD.	ERIK.
He didn't tell me details…	No—guys, I don't even remember it, there's nothing to tell…

BRIGID.	DEIRDRE.
Well, now I don't believe you…	I saw the way you woke up, don't tell me you can't remember somethin'—

RICHARD. *(Defending Erik.)*	ERIK. *(Smiling, to Brigid.)*
Hey, no I forget mine if I don't write them down in the morning…	[Man, you're a piece of work.]

ERIK. See?… there you go…

DEIRDRE. Well whatever it was, couldn't a been scarier than the— *(Laughing.)* I made him watch this—what was it called, Erik?… / the movie…?

ERIK. What?

DEIRDRE. … the Lifetime movie about the housewife who got AIDS, / guys—it was so cheesy but really terrifying…

BRIGID.	ERIK.
Mom, you're steamrolling the—	She made me watch that…
	(To Brigid.) Worst two hours
	of my life…

DEIRDRE. You loved it.

RICHARD. What was scary about it?

DEIRDRE. This housewife cheats on her husband, right?—and he comes home from work and asks her how her day was and—I mean what can she say? "Today I cheated on you and contracted the HIV virus, honey, how was *your* day?"… Can you *imagine*?

BRIGID. You're trying to be a comedian, no more wine for you—

RICHARD. No, she's fine—be nicer to your mom, babe.

DEIRDRE. Thanks, Rich.

> *Brigid goes to the kitchen, frustrated. Rich follows her. We can glimpse them having a controlled-but-heated conversation. Erik raises his eyebrows, tries to make light of this.*

Anything I say makes her [annoyed]…

ERIK. Yeah? Well who does she remind you of?

DEIRDRE. You.

ERIK.	DEIRDRE.
Me? She's all *you*,	*You*, yeah you,
my friend…	my friend…

> *They smile at this disagreement.*

DEIRDRE. Don't wait until after dinner.

> *Erik drinks his beer, thinks.*

(Getting up.) Your call, Big Guy…

Deirdre heads for the stairs. Brigid returns from the kitchen alley.

BRIGID. Where're you going?

DEIRDRE. Gonna check on Aimee—

BRIGID. I'll do it, stay down… stay down…

ERIK. Are her shakes in the fridge?

BRIGID. Yeah—Rich'll get it, sit down. Rich can you bring out an Ensure shake? The straws are in the bag.

RICHARD. No problem.

ERIK. Thanks.

> *Brigid goes upstairs. Rich returns with an Ensure shake. Erik opens it, prepares the drink for Momo under the following. A bit awkward with just Erik, Deirdre, and Rich:*

DEIRDRE. So how's school, what is it a, a master's in social work you'll get?

RICHARD. Yeah, I have one more year…

Upstairs: *Brigid knocks on the bathroom door.*

BRIGID. You need anything?

AIMEE. *(O.S.)* An air freshener…?

BRIGID. Just stink the place up. We'll deal.

AIMEE. *(O.S.)* I'll be out in a few.	***Downstairs:*** MOMO. *(Barely audible.)* I'm I here'm I why'm I heresuh blag sezzor why'm I sezzor… *(A bit louder.)* I'm I here'm I / why'm I heresuh blag sezzor why'm I sezzor…

45

Downstairs:

ERIK. You're here 'cause it's Thanksgiving, Mom, that's why you're here, Brigid invited us…

> *Rich continues dinner preparations during the following conversation.*

RICHARD. Brigid said you guys went on a cruise last summer?

DEIRDRE. Yeah, we've gone on four of 'em now, to Halifax and Mexico… you ever been on one?

> ***Upstairs****: Brigid pauses at the top of the staircase to listen…*

RICHARD. Uh, not on one of those big ships, but… I sailed with my family growing up.

ERIK. We try to get the girls to come but they think it's pretty lame, you know?

DEIRDRE. Yeah, we know it's cheesy but we like it 'cause they take care of everything, you feel taken care of…

RICHARD. Yeah, I get that. Are you able to avoid all of the touristy stuff when you dock? / Or do you—

DEIRDRE. All of the… well, they let you off in good spots usually… where there's a lot to do…?

RICHARD. Oh, cool…

DEIRDRE. … Yeah…

> *Small beat.*

… the spots are pretty good usually… where they leave you off at.

> ***Upstairs****: Brigid is still listening to this conversation. It makes her sad.*

RICHARD. Cool, cool… I tend to be more of a… I like to wander off the beaten path…

DEIRDRE. No, I hear you… Brigid's the same way…

RICHARD. Can I [pour you more wine]…?

DEIRDRE. Thanks…

Beat.

There's usually decent entertainment options on the ship, lotta the singers have professional credits. Lotta stuff going on all at once…

RICHARD.	ERIK.
Sounds awesome.	Yeah, yeah, so at night she can go see a show and I can go, you, know go do / something else…

DEIRDRE. Gamble. You gamble.

ERIK. Or whatever else I feel / like doing…

DEIRDRE. Well c'mon, don't act like you play shuffleboard on the lido deck.

> *Upstairs: Brigid finally heads downstairs. Erik, going upstairs, passes her.*

BRIGID. Hey…

ERIK. Just gonna check the score of the game…

BRIGID. Okay…

Upstairs:	*Downstairs:*
Erik climbs the stairs, struggles for reception by the window.	DEIRDRE. *(Pushing the Ensure shake closer.)* Mom, you're not hungry? Just finish drinking your—
He sees some falling ashes. It looks like light flurries.	
Perhaps the smallest suggestion of a moving shadow in the alley.	*Momo overturns her Ensure shake, splattering it everywhere.*

Erik's a bit unsettled by what he sees. He steps away from the window, takes a few calming deep breaths...

MOMO.
Sorn it all /... sorn it all sezzor dollen black? Homeran sinitz inner therell... sornitz allinners ... sorn it allinners...

She mumbles under the following:

DEIRDRE. Oh man... I got it, you're alright, Mom... *(Calling up.)* Erik...

BRIGID. Mom, let him go, I got it—we have loads of paper towels...

RICHARD. Where are they?

BRIGID.
They're in the shopping bag upstairs, Rich can you—I got it, Mom...

MOMO.
... sinnin... sahn... airy-wheres... itsen... senna...

Downstairs: Brigid cleans up the mess, back and forth between the kitchen, soaking up the liquid and wringing out her kitchen towel in the sink, while Deirdre wheels Momo away from the mess and into the other downstairs room, calming her.

Upstairs: Rich arrives upstairs, passes Erik.

RICHARD.
We had a minor spill...

MOMO. *(Tapering to quiet.)*
sinnin... sahn... airywheres ... itsen... senna... sahn... airywheres... itsen... senna...

DEIRDRE. *(To Momo.)* There you go...

Upstairs: Rich gets the paper towels in the next room. He comes back towards the stairs and stops, seeing Erik is still staring out the window.

RICHARD. ... You okay?

ERIK. Uh, yeah, just worried about the roads. It's snowing out there…

RICHARD. *(Looking out the window.)* Oh. No, I think someone from a higher floor just emptied their ashtray.

> ***Downstairs***: *Deirdre has been helping Momo up and onto the couch.*

DEIRDRE. There we go… / there we go…

> ***Upstairs:***

ERIK. Hey make sure you get blinds up, will you? You don't want people looking in on you…

RICHARD. Yeah, no I'm on it, this week I'll put some up.

> *Richard descends the staircase with the paper towels.*

> ***Downstairs:***

DEIRDRE. You feeling good, Mom?… Now you can rest… there you go…

Upstairs:	DEIRDRE. *(Seeing Richard*
Aimee exits the bathroom, phone	*clean up the last of the spill.)*
in hand. A bit nervous, she makes	Thanks, Rich… we got most
a call. She doesn't know Erik is	of it…
in the next room.	

RICHARD. Okay, no problem…

> ***Downstairs***: *Richard heads to the kitchen. Brigid's back is to us, her hands on the sink counter. She wrings out the towel, appears to be de-stressing, taking a moment for herself.*

AIMEE. *(On her cell.)* Hey, hi… Happy—I know—Happy Thanksgiving—
I know, but—
I know, I know…

BRIGID. Ahhh… [will we make it through dinner?]

RICHARD.
Can I get you anything?

AIMEE.
Uh-huh…

BRIGID.
Can I get *you* anything?

… Mm-hm…

> ***Downstairs****: Richard kisses Brigid, she smiles, he pulls her further into the kitchen alley…*

> ***Upstairs****: Aimee continues her phone conversation. In the next room, Erik listens.*

AIMEE. I know, I know, I just thought the holidays could be an exception…
… uh-huh… well sorry if—
I understand, I just wanted to hear your—
no I get it, I get it…
I'm good, you know?, I'm okay… and you're, are you upstate with the fam, or?…
(Hurt, but not showing it.) … oh… no, I figured you were seeing someone… I saw your pics online—
no I think it's good… I've been dating too… so…
yeah, nothing serious, but…

> ***Downstairs****:*
> BRIGID. *(Calling from the kitchen.)*
> Mom, does Momo need another shake?

AIMEE.
… yeah, yeah…

DEIRDRE. Sure, let's give it a try…

> *Brigid gets a shake out of the fridge, then disappears in the kitchen alley to find a straw.*

> ***Upstairs****: Erik moves in a bit closer, listening to Aimee's phone conversation.*

AIMEE. … Well hey, I'll let you go, but glad you're—
… ha, I'll tell them, they'll appreciate that… so—
absolutely, and love to your—
exactly, Happy Thanksgiving and—

(Hurt, but trying to keep things light.) —well don't wish me a Merry Chr—
we can talk again before *Christmas...*

Downstairs:

DEIRDRE. *(Laying Momo on the couch.)* There you go... there you go...

Deirdre steps away from Momo to tell Bridget to forget the Ensure shake and catches a glimpse of Rich and Brigid enjoying a quiet moment—they're just visible in the kitchen alley. They are laughing about something. Rich kisses Brigid's forehead, then slaps her on the ass playfully. Richard disappears into the alley as Brigid slaps his ass back. This stirs something inside Deirdre. She retreats back to the couch.

AIMEE.
... uh-huh...

... yeah...

... uh-huh...

... uh-huh...

AIMEE. *(Successfully fighting back tears.)* ... huh, uh-huh... well maybe your therapist is right...
mm-hm... Just, the holidays feel... *wrong*,
without us at least—[talking]...
—no, I respect that...
yeah... Well look, love to all your—
... you too...
I will, I'll tell them...
okay, you too... bye...

Aimee hangs up. Erik knocks on the entryway.

ERIK. Hey...

Aimee cries, unable to hold it in. Erik holds her.

AIMEE. Ugh... I miss her...

ERIK. Hey...

AIMEE. ... All the time...

ERIK. ... We know...

> *Downstairs: Brigid brings Deirdre and Momo a new Ensure shake with a freshly rinsed straw. But Momo is now half-asleep.*

DEIRDRE. We'll try later, she's gonna sleep for a bit I bet...

> *Deirdre adjusts Momo's head, maybe with a memory-foam travel pillow they always take with them. Brigid returns the shake to the kitchen. Rich abandons dinner preparations and emerges from the kitchen alley with the bottle of wine.*

> *Upstairs:*

AIMEE.
Gimme a sec...

RICHARD. *(Re: the wine.)*
May I...

DEIRDRE. Thanks, yeah...

BRIGID.
I wish you knew her before she got sick, Rich...

Aimee breaks her embrace with Erik. She goes to the bathroom to get some toilet paper to wipe her nose/dry her tears.

DEIRDRE.
She was somethin', she refused to quit driving, Rich, *refused*, but... six years ago?, Erik couldn't bring himself to take the keys from her, so he got her to take a driver's exam so the decision wouldn't be on him, and part of the test is—They show her a picture of a yield sign, but without the word "yield" on it... Well she can't name it, but enough of her's still there that she goes to the poor guy giving the test, really pissed off, she goes: "Trust me, I'd know what to do if I was driving." And he's like, "Then just tell me what you'd do if

Erik uses the moment alone to wander down the hallway and stretch out his lower back, which is bothering him.

He eventually is drawn back to the window, inspects the alley.

you were driving and pulled up to this sign." And she goes, "I'd see what everyone else was doing, then I'd do that."

He stares out the window, rubbing his lower back.

Rich smiles.

BRIGID. Where're you at with the whole... nursing home discussion?...

DEIRDRE. Mom's—as long as Uncle John can watch her weekdays, we're fine—

BRIGID.
I want you guys to [take care of yourselves]—

RICHARD.
I love that—oh... I was just gonna say I love that you and Erik both call her "Mom."

DEIRDRE. Well, that's what she is to me, that's what's special about marriage, Rich, *real* marriage... you get two families.

BRIGID. *("Give it a rest, Mom...")* Okay...

RICHARD. I'm very committed to Brigid.

> **Upstairs**: *Aimee exits the bathroom, spies Erik rubbing his lower back.*

AIMEE. Hey...

DEIRDRE. I'm glad, that's good...

AIMEE. Big Guy, how's your back...?

ERIK. How's my back?, how's *your* back?

AIMEE. [That's a great point, Dad,] you doing your exercises?

ERIK. Yeah, yeah...

> **Downstairs**: *Momo dozes off on the couch.*

BRIGID. So it's okay if she sleeps here?

ERIK. You'll find someone new...

DEIRDRE. Oh yeah, the meds she's on—she gets in three good naps a day...

> *Deirdre helps adjust Momo on the couch.*

ERIK. I mean it, hey, I'm serious, you're gonna find someone new—

AIMEE. Not with *history*—Carol knew me with *acne*... she helped me with my law school application...

ERIK. You're gonna come outta this stronger, / I promise.

AIMEE. Stop, Dad, stop lying to me.

> *Beat.*

Don't *actually* stop, keep saying things to me...

DEIRDRE. Where's her blanket?

ERIK. Whattya want me to... Momo'd... if I skinned my knee or had any kinda setback, Momo'd say... "This, too, shall pass," / and I'd roll my eyes at her, but... this'll pass, it will...

BRIGID. *(Finding Momo's blanket.)* Here...

DEIRDRE. Thanks... there we go...

RICHARD. *(To Brigid.)* So turkey's out... I won't carve until we're all down here, yeah?	AIMEE. Ugh... I need some more... bathroom time, I'll be down, okay?
	ERIK. Yeah...

BRIGID. *(Calling upstairs.)* Dad! Aimee!

Upstairs: Aimee returns to the bathroom. Erik heads for the stairs.

Downstairs: Deirdre is lovingly setting up Momo on the couch.

DEIRDRE. She's calm now, Rich, but... man—when she has a fit, it's like watching her turn into someone else, you know?...

RICHARD. Can I help you get her [situated]...?

DEIRDRE. Yeah, just, lift her feet there...

> *Richard moves her feet into a more comfortable position. Erik is on his way downstairs.*

ERIK. Hey, get your hands off of my mother, / you bastard!—

RICHARD.
Oh my God I was just—

BRIGID.
Dad—stop—
(To Richard.) He's teasing you...

ERIK. *(Smiling.)* The Lions are up ten.

BRIGID. Your sense of humor is terrible.

DEIRDRE. Have you guys noticed that *everyone's* sense of humor is terrible except for Brigid's? / How interesting...

ERIK.
Score one for Mom!

RICHARD.
Amen, yes...

DEIRDRE.
How's Aimee?

BRIGID.
Not funny.

ERIK. Give her five minutes, she's okay... *(Deirdre isn't convinced.)* ... she's okay...

DEIRDRE. I was telling Rich, before we got her on these new meds... you coulda put some of her worst outbursts in a horror flick.

ERIK. Brigid's? / I agree...

BRIGID. Dad!

Richard finds this joke pretty funny. Brigid laughs too.

DEIRDRE. … I'm serious, I keep seeing ads for that zombie show on TV… it's awful, but it makes me think of / Mom's worst [tantrums]—

ERIK. Yeah, but we're doing okay, right? We're okay…

DEIRDRE. Yeah, with the help of God, yeah…

Small beat.

… [I] can't believe people wanna watch that stuff at night / when there's—

BRIGID. She hates anything with blood or gore—

DEIRDRE. —Yeah, well there's enough going on in the real world to give me the creeps, / I don't need any more…

RICHARD. That's like—I bet she'd appreciate—there's this comic book called *Quasar*… I was obsessed with it as a kid, / it's about this—

BRIGID. You're *still* obsessed with / *Quasar*, he won't throw them out…

RICHARD. Yes I am, be quiet—it's about this species of like half-alien, half-demon creatures with teeth on their backs—

BRIGID.	RICHARD.
Oh my God… just call them monsters—	—but on their planet—

RICHARD. —on their planet, the scary stories they tell each other… they're all about us. The horror stories for the monsters are all about humans. / I love that…

DEIRDRE. *(To Rich.)*	BRIGID. *(Joking, to Erik.)*
Yeah well people are [terrifying]… you should meet my boss… no teeth on his back, but man…	Thank God he's in grad school…

BRIGID. But monsters aren't *scared* of us, / so why would—

RICHARD. Sure they are, it's always a man driving a stake through the heart of the vampire—or if you're a zombie, you eat people but your biggest threat is what?—getting killed by some enterprising human, / right?

DEIRDRE. I get it, Rich…

BRIGID. They'd be more scared by monster-eating monsters or something, am I right?

ERIK. Monsters aren't real so it's a weird thing to wanna be right about.

RICHARD.	DEIRDRE.
That's probably the soundest argument.	Yeah… well…
	… that's not what you thought last night… you thought *that* was pretty real… there's sweat on the sheets to prove it…

ERIK. *(Smiling.)* Wow, you can't let that go, / can you?

DEIRDRE. Well tell me what you dreamed / and I'll drop it…

ERIK. Well you're assuming I saw something specific when she was just— / It wasn't like that, okay?

BRIGID. Wait wait "she"?—So you *do* remember something specific / about your dream—

ERIK.	DEIRDRE.
Oh man, you guys're relentless…	Erik, have you been dreaming about a supermodel this whole time?—
Rich, help me out here…	

RICHARD. *(Teasing.)* Sorry, man, I tell Brigid my dreams all the time…

BRIGID. Yes you do, all of them…

RICHARD.
—Two weeks ago, I dreamt my
oldest sister was a mannequin   BRIGID.
working in a grocery store…   … Richard…
What, I'm serious…

DEIRDRE.   ERIK.
Was yours that [weird]?—   All I remember…
Oh… what…?

ERIK. … There's not much to…

BRIGID. Tell us… come on, Big Guy…

ERIK. … A coupla nights I've had this [recurring dream]…
… there'll be a, a woman…

BRIGID. Uh-huh… and…

ERIK. *(Trying to remember.)* … her back's to me… or maybe…
something happens where…
her head turns, and
I can see that her face is all… [messed up]

DEIRDRE.   BRIGID.
What?   Just tell us—

ERIK. … Her skin's stretched over her eyes and her mouth…

BRIGID. Ewww…

DEIRDRE. She's got no face?

ERIK. … Just skin where her eyes and mouth should be, / you
know—

BRIGID. Ewwwww—

58

ERIK. —Yeah, over the holes in her ears—

A THUD from above. Everyone jumps—

Whoa, / whoa, how's that for timing? What the hell is going on up there?…

RICHARD.
Okay, okay… yeah, maybe we *should* go up and say something…

BRIGID.
Guys, sorry about that—

DEIRDRE.
What do you think she's—is she exercising up there, do you think?…

Welcome to New York…

ERIK. No, you think she's sweatin' to the oldies up there? / No way…

DEIRDRE. Oh wait, you know what it probably is? / I'm just realizing…

BRIGID.
What is it?

RICHARD.
What?

DEIRDRE. … It's the faceless lady, telling us to be quiet… / or maybe she wants some turkey…

ERIK.
Nice… very funny…

BRIGID.
Mom… are you drunk?…

In fact everyone has had just enough to drink that this starts to feel very funny.

DEIRDRE. *(Fighting back laughter.)* —But how would she eat the turkey? She's got no mouth…

Deirdre mimes a woman without a mouth trying to eat turkey. It's so unfunny it's kind of funny. Eventually even Brigid laughs.

ERIK.
I'm so glad I shared my nightmare, thank you for your love and support—

BRIGID.
Oh my God, *stop*… Tell us the rest…

DEIRDRE. We're teasing!

RICHARD. Tough crowd, Erik…

BRIGID. Finish telling us your—

ERIK.	DEIRDRE.
Oh right, like I'm gonna—	I'm sorry, I'm sorry…
you had your chance—	oh don't punish us, I'm
yeah *now* you're sorry…	just being silly, I'm sorry…
man, you see what I'm up	how does it end?
against, Rich?	

> ***Upstairs**: Aimee calls from the top of the stairs.*

AIMEE. Should I ask the dinosaur upstairs to tread a little more softly?

BRIGID. *(Calling up.)* Not unless you speak Cantonese… / just come down…

RICHARD. Erik you'll appreciate this… last week I dreamed I fell through an ice cream cone made of grass and became a baby.

BRIGID. Okay, no no no, save your dreams for Christmas, we're almost ready to eat here… *(Calling up.)* … Aimee!…

> ***Upstairs**: From the apartment above them, the sound of running footsteps moving from one side of the room to the other. Aimee looks up. So does Erik. It's a bizarre noise—maybe the kind a tantrum-throwing toddler would make stomping about.*

ERIK. Why don't I go up and ask her to just please /—just to please keep it down—

BRIGID. No, no these floors are so old, Dad—hey, sit down…

	RICHARD.
Brigid runs up the stairs.	The whole building groans at times…
	we have two sets of ear plugs.

> ***Upstairs**: Aimee is responding to an email on her phone.*

Brigid starts stomping around.

AIMEE. What are you doing?

BRIGID. Showing Dad how creaky the floors are…

ERIK. Okay… you don't have to do that!

> *Aimee starts jumping around with her. At a certain point the jumping and stomping becomes more about Aimee and Brigid releasing a lot of stress.*

Downstairs:

DEIRDRE.
These floors are made of
tissue paper…

RICHARD. *(Calling up.)*
Okay honey, point proven!

> **Upstairs**: *They recover. Brigid playfully collapses on the floor, a bit exhausted. Aimee moves closer to the window for reception.*

AIMEE. *(To her BlackBerry, re: a new message.)*
Stop emailing me…

Downstairs:
RICHARD.
Water and soda for dinner?

ERIK.
Both—for the both of us, yeah?

DEIRDRE.
Yeah, thanks…

Rich is in the kitchen.

BRIGID. *(This has been on her mind.)*
Did you see the Mary statue?… and she's bringing up marriage… we've been doing so good, I dunno why she's back to—

AIMEE. *(Half-engaged with her email.)*
Being here's just… making it more *real* for her, no?

Deirdre checks in with Erik about something; Erik nods, then wanders into the adjoining room and paces.

BRIGID.
No, I dunno, something's
[not right…] I dunno…

AIMEE. *(Putting her BlackBerry away.)*
… sorry—they even find me on holidays… It never ends…

… How's work for *you?*…

Deirdre decides to give Erik his space; she moves into the kitchen to help Rich.

DEIRDRE.
How can I help, Rich?

RICHARD.
Uh, how about…

BRIGID. Uh, the restaurant pays me under the table so I can still collect unemployment, so that's been good… but… my *career* is… [non-existent…] [I don't wanna talk about it…]

AIMEE. Hey, okay…

Brigid takes a deep breath, exhales.

BRIGID. I'm just glad Rich and I made the leap, / it was time, you know?

AIMEE.
Yeah… he's great, Bridge…

BRIGID.
Yeah, we were always at each other's place, so financially it was just stupid, you know… Rich made up this list of pros and cons… to move in or not to move in… Aimee, his *lists*… I found one posted to the fridge last week called "Ways to Have Fun"; [What the fuck?!]—stuff like: dance with yourself; take long walks at sunset… game nights…

Downstairs*:*
Deirdre continues to help Rich in the kitchen. They are occasionally half-heard speaking to each other.

Erik is the prominent figure downstairs—he paces in the hall, refers to a piece of paper.

AIMEE. That's endearing…

BRIGID. I know…

> *Audible-but-indecipherable conversation between Deirdre and Richard in the kitchen alley.*

… I dunno, we were happy without making it so official, so /… I dunno…

AIMEE. Yeah, well… Carol and I broke up because… we were unhappy?… And now I'm [wondering]… Maybe loving someone long-term is more about… deciding whether to go through life unhappy alone… or unhappy with someone else?

BRIGID. Richard can draw up a list of reasons why your breakup was a good thing, if you want… / I can ask him to draft a very long list—

AIMEE. No, shuttup so… ugh: I need to have that surgery… / the one where they'll—

BRIGID. What? I thought you could put that off until your sixties or—

AIMEE. This test showed—it's just dysplasia which means… it's not cancer, but with colitis it'll become cancer if they don't take it out, so…

BRIGID. You'll lose the whole intestine?

AIMEE. It cures the disease, though, so… but… yeah… they make a hole in your abdomen so the waste can, you know…

BRIGID. Do Mom and Dad know?

AIMEE. No, I don't want to discuss it at dinner and… I'm okay, I'm mostly just like… uhhhh, how am I gonna find another girl-friend?… / I'm serious…

BRIGID. You're a complete catch.

AIMEE. I'm gonna be pooing out of a hole in my abdomen. Who's gonna date me?

BRIGID. Lots of people…

AIMEE. Lotta *ugly* people…

BRIGID. Aimee!

AIMEE. … lotta troll ladies, who'll have their own troll problems…

BRIGID. Stop…

AIMEE. … living under bridges…

BRIGID. … If you shat out your ears—if they rerouted your colon to your *ears* I'd still marry you.

AIMEE. Uh-huh… when do I even—do I wait until the third date to be, like: "Just FYI, I shit out of a hole in my belly." Is that a fifth-date thing?

BRIGID. Sorry you have to go through all that.

> ***Downstairs****: Audible-but-indecipherable talk between Richard and Deirdre in the kitchen alley.*
> *Erik resolves to go upstairs, but stops near the top of the staircase when he realizes the girls are talking about him.*

AIMEE. I'm more worried about—did you notice Mom's knees?… Going down / the stairs…

BRIGID. I saw, yeah… I'm afraid to ask how her arthritis is… or Dad's back… / I don't wanna know…

AIMEE. Well it's bothering him—can't you tell he's—

BRIGID. No, yeah, do you think it's because… he hasn't been sleeping, right?…

Upstairs: The light fixture above Brigid and Aimee burns out.

AIMEE.
Was that the light?

BRIGID.
Shit…

> *Downstairs: Erik shifts his direction and heads back downstairs, hurt by what he's overheard.*

DEIRDRE. What are they doing up there?—

ERIK.
They're comin', they're comin'… *(Aside, to Deirdre.)* I'll talk to them after dinner… I'll talk to them later…

BRIGID. *(Calling down.)* Richard… Rich… babe, do we have a spare bulb? The light up here is out.

RICHARD. *(Calling up.)* Can you just… open the bathroom door, let that light spill into—

BRIGID. Richard, that's not a very good solution to the problem—

RICHARD. Well, I'm not a magician, do you want me / to make a light bulb appear out of thin air?

DEIRDRE. Well hey, how—Rich… how 'bout, there's an LED lantern in our care package… lemme get that out so it's not like a cave up there… Problem solved…

RICHARD. Uh, sure… thanks, Deirdre.

> *Deirdre goes upstairs.*
> *Brigid turns on the light in the bathroom and opens the door;*
> *Aimee opens the care package box.*

BRIGID. You bought us a *lantern*?

ERIK. *(Calling up.)* *I* bought it. After what the hurricane did to this neighborhood… you can't be without light, not in a basement apartment. They say another storm's gonna strike this year… you're in a Zone A flood zone.

> *Downstairs: Richard takes care of final table arrangements.*

Upstairs: Deirdre and Aimee and Brigid sift through her care package box.

AIMEE. Cans of tuna? Oh Mom…

DEIRDRE. You gotta be prepared…

Downstairs:

RICHARD. I don't blame you for worrying, especially after—Brigid told me about… you and Aimee.

ERIK.
Yeah, well…

… yeah…

… what's funny is Bridge is the one who'd been—you can imagine her as a teenager, she was a piece a work, she loved teasing me because Scranton's a stone's throw from the greatest city in the world but I've never even, you know, I'd never seen the Statue of Liberty, never seen the… [anyway…]

… She's a piece of work… [anyway…]

… So when—
Aimee got a, an interview to be a paralegal at this New York firm… I took the day off, drove her in… Aimee's at her interview by 8:45, thirty-seventh floor and… I'm at a Dunkin' Donuts across the street 'cause the observation deck didn't open until 9:30, / otherwise…

Upstairs:
BRIGID.
There are literally three thousand double-A batteries in here.

DEIRDRE.
There are literally twelve.

Deirdre puts batteries into the two flashlights and the lantern. Aimee wanders away to deal with work emails.

BRIGID.
A wind-up radio?…

DEIRDRE.
You'll thank me later.

RICHARD.
Oh man...

ERIK.
... Yeah, took me hours to
find her 'cause... I had no
cell then... but...

RICHARD.
Man, I can't even [imagine]...
/ it's just crazy...

ERIK.
... Yeah... well... what's crazy
is how you still mess up...
... It's crazy how you still—

BRIGID. *(To Aimee.)*
Stop checking your email.

DEIRDRE. *(Turning on the
lantern.)*
There we go...

*Deirdre walks into the darkest
spot in the upstairs hallway to
place the lantern on the floor.
Brigid is about to head back
downstairs...*

Upstairs: *Deirdre SCREAMS. Her lantern falls to the floor.*

Downstairs: *Richard and Erik run for the stairs.*

RICHARD.
Hey you okay?

ERIK.
What? / What's wrong?

DEIRDRE.   It was a rat or something... oh God... where did it
go? / Did you see it?

*Brigid shines her flashlight on the floor. Erik and Richard arrive
upstairs.*

Downstairs: *Momo wakes up, stumbles off the couch, slowly
plods to the kitchen...*

ERIK.
What's wrong you okay? /
What happened?

AIMEE.
Oh my God I absoutely
saw that what was that?!?

BRIGID.
Okay don't scream—
American cockroaches are huge...
I'm sure it was just a cockroach—

RICHARD.
Okay, okay, I'll get it...

DEIRDRE. I have nothing to stand on… someone give me something to stand on…

BRIGID. It was an American cockroach, they're huge / okay?— don't get so upset—

AIMEE. Ewwwww…

DEIRDRE. A cockroach the size of a mouse *is* upsetting!

AIMEE. Ahhhh, I can't be up here right now… no, Mom, c'mon…	DEIRDRE. Shouldn't we kill it?

BRIGID. I'm not killing it…	RICHARD. *(Laughing.)* I'll get it if it comes back…

DEIRDRE. *(Laughing.)* Don't laugh at me…

> **Upstairs**: *The cockroach-melee winds down.*

ERIK. *(To Richard.)* You gotta caulk. If you let me caulk and put down some boric acid…	BRIGID. Okay, okay… everyone retreat… it's just a cockroach…
RICHARD. I hear you, Erik, I will… okay, everyone down for dinner, sorry for the bug scare…	DEIRDRE. Jesus, Mary, and Joseph…

> *Erik descends the stairs and doesn't see Momo. Richard places the lit lantern deep in the recesses of the hallway, or the darkest nook upstairs. The lantern's light isn't in clear view; a box or piece of architecture obscures it.*

AIMEE. *(To Brigid.)* I had roaches in my first Philly apartment…

DEIRDRE. I should have included insect traps in the care package—

ERIK. Mom… *Mom…?* Hey where's… Dee, where's Mom?…

> *Erik checks outside the basement door; no sign of Momo.*

... help me look for her!
Just look!

DEIRDRE.
Well where could she—you want me to look under the *couch*, where the hell could she be?!

A CRASH of a few empty pots and pans from the kitchen alley. Erik disappears into the kitchen alley. Momo mumbles under the following scene as Erik helps her back to the couch and everyone tries to recover.

MOMO. *(O.S.)*
... nairywheres do we blag werstrus, doll sezzer big sussten back... sezz it whairidoll... er hairin sildern fernal garn ackening ery or loddinsezz...

ERIK. *(O.S.)*
... Mom... / Jesus Christ...

AIMEE.
What? Is she hurt?

DEIRDRE.
Is she okay?

BRIGID.
What happened? Is she okay?

ERIK. *(O.S.)*
... Jesus Christ... yeah, God...

Aimee, Richard, and Brigid arrive downstairs. Erik returns, guiding Momo back to her wheelchair. Deirdre helps. Momo is fine.

ERIK. ... yeah, she's okay, she almost burnt herself on the stove, God...

DEIRDRE. You were more scared than she was, you okay? / You're okay, Mom...

ERIK. Yeah, I shouldn't have left her...

AIMEE. She's okay /... I'll clean up in here...

BRIGID.
You okay Big Guy?

ERIK.
I know, I know...
Yeah, I'm alright...

DEIRDRE.
Why don't we give her her
other pill before we eat...

RICHARD.
I'll take care of the
kitchen...

BRIGID. It's just some pots and pans, Dad, no worries...

Deirdre helps Erik with Momo. Erik gives her a pill.

RICHARD. We definitely owe you guys for that care package, clearly we needed it.

ERIK. Yeah, you did, and cell phone flashlights don't last long in a blackout. You gotta be prepared...

AIMEE.
Cut them a break, Dad—

Because for me—hey—hey—
hey, I'm telling you what I think,
I think it means the two of us
were in New York on a terrible
morning. / That's all...

ERIK.
... and I still don't get how you
can live here after— *(To Aimee.)*
—or that it hasn't sent you back
to church—don't you think sur-
vivin' that day means *somethin*?

ERIK. That's it?

AIMEE.
Yes, Dad, that's it.

BRIGID.
Yeah, me too—I'm not scared
of coincidences—

DEIRDRE. Me too, they're not scary if you believe in some kinda God, / God doesn't make mistakes...

BRIGID. That, yeah, that wasn't my point, Sneaky—

AIMEE. Alright, Momo's okay, yeah? /... That's what matters...

DEIRDRE.
Thank God, yes...

ERIK.
Yeah, man, you gave me a
scare, Mom, / you really did...

Erik kisses Momo.

BRIGID. So, should—should we bring her wheelchair to the table for dinner?

DEIRDRE. No, no she'll be sleeping soon...

BRIGID. Does the medicine make her sleep?—should you be—

ERIK. It just calms her down—we can bring her to the table, / see how she feels—

BRIGID. Yeah, don't knock her out / just because—

DEIRDRE. Hey, if you want to come home more and help control her tantrums then you can judge the way we care for her.

BRIGID. I'm not trying to judge you I just want—can't you hire someone / to help with—?

DEIRDRE. It'd cost a hundred bucks a night to hire someone to watch her, *a hundred bucks* to make sure she doesn't fall / and get hurt—

ERIK. Hey... okay—

DEIRDRE. No, she needs to think before she opens her mouth.

BRIGID. Sorry.

Erik attends to Momo. Brigid focuses her energy in the kitchen.

AIMEE. *(Half-volume, to Deirdre.)* Let's all just... [calm down...]	BRIGID. Do we need anything else, Rich?
	RICHARD. No we're good, babe... you okay?
... God bless us, everyone...	
	BRIGID. Yeah... how's the turkey?
DEIRDRE. Yeah, yeah...	

RICHARD. It's great—will everybody eat dark meat? / Or just—

AIMEE. We'll eat it all, Rich, / just send it our way…

ERIK. *(This is a funny question.)* Will we eat dark meat?

DEIRDRE. Yeah but—I will, I'm just… oh man, I'm just… I'm back on Weight Watchers / and man…

AIMEE. That's great, Mom…

DEIRDRE. … Thanks, yeah… it's tough, one baby ice cream cone takes up half my points for the day… Same for a junior cheeseburger at Wendy's, it's tough staying on track.

BRIGID. Especially if you eat a bucket of ranch dip before dinner.

AIMEE. [Don't say stuff like that…]

> *Richard returns from the kitchen area, sets down final side dishes. He isn't aware of how wounded Deirdre is at this moment. Erik is also unaware as he arrives at the table. Momo is awake but doesn't seem very alert.*

DEIRDRE. *(To Brigid.)* I'm, uh, not being careful with points today, / not on holidays…

RICHARD. … This is the last side dish, yeah? Think we're good to go— / Are we ready…?

AIMEE. Uh-huh… / let's eat…

ERIK. *(Sitting down, gesturing for them to hold hands.)* Okay… hands…

> *They bow their heads, hold hands for grace. Richard doesn't know the grace but participates in the hand-holding.*

Bless us oh Lord…

ERIK, AIMEE, BRIGID, DEIRDRE, and MOMO. … and these Thy gifts, which we are about to receive, from Thy bounty, through Christ our Lord, Amen.

They have all noticed that Momo joined in. They smile, thrilled.

ERIK. Did you / hear that?

BRIGID.	AIMEE.
Momo, I'm so glad you're here!	Amazing…

ERIK. Is it crazy if we do it again? Just / one more time…

They all ad lib no…

AIMEE. … No, go for it.

ERIK. *(Smiling, holding their hands again.)* Bless us oh Lord…

Momo joins in again.

ERIK, AIMEE, BRIGID, DEIRDRE, and MOMO. … and these Thy gifts, which we are about to receive, from Thy bounty, through Christ our Lord, Amen.

> *This time they all spontaneously clap, Momo does too. They laugh at their impulse to applaud an old woman for saying grace.*

ERIK. Mom, you remember Aimee and Brigid, these are your granddaughters…

> *Momo picks up the serving spoon in the sweet potatoes and is about to take a bite—Erik catches her in time, removes the serving spoon from her hand…*

AIMEE.	BRIGID.
Don't put the spotlight on her…	We're happy you're here, Momes. Guys, dig in, don't wait…

They start to eat, pass the food around the table.

ERIK. Wow, all looks great.

Everyone ad libs agreement.

DEIRDRE. This looks good, what's this…

BRIGID. It's a rainbow chard salad, it's packed with nutrients… everything else is familiar, I think…

DEIRDRE. You guys did a great job…

RICHARD.   ERIK.
Thanks.   Awesome.

> *Beat. They eat.*

MOMO. Dig a hole shower.

> *They all laugh at the randomness of the remark.*

ERIK. This is definitely not one of your better days, Mom… oh man, we, uh… we'll all be there someday, right?… / We love you so much, Mom…

AIMEE.   RICHARD.
Yes we will be…   Dig in, everybody, please…

> *They eat.*

DEIRDRE. This turkey is so moist, / good job guys…

ERIK. Mm-hmm…

MOMO. Shower in holes.

> *They all stifle laughter, acknowledge the remark; it's funny, but also a little upsetting.*
> *They eat.*
> *Aimee starts laughing.*

ERIK. What?

AIMEE. Momo's Christmas toast…

> *They all start laughing. Richard doesn't know what this inside joke is.*

BRIGID. On Christmas, Momo—she always delivers a traditional Irish toast, it's ancient, right?

ERIK. It's ancient and it's beautiful, but one year Aimee's mind was in the gutter—

AIMEE. I was twelve!

BRIGID. And ever since the blessing sounds kinda dirty to us—

DEIRDRE.	ERIK.
Not to us…	To *you guys* it sounds dirty…

RICHARD. What's the blessing?

AIMEE. "May the Virgin and her Child lift your latch on Christmas night."

> *Some wine dribbles out of Richard's mouth; he wasn't expecting to find it that funny.*

DEIRDRE.	AIMEE.
Not you too, Rich…	I know, right?! They don't get it…

ERIK. We *get* it we just don't agree…

DEIRDRE. … I first thought latch-lifting was a kinda sexual position…

BRIGID.	DEIRDRE.
Ewww, Mom…	… I'm serious, thought maybe it was like scissoring, or / somethin'—

Mom! / Eeewwww…

AIMEE. Oh my God Mom, I'm never telling you anything again, / we're not discussing this at the table.

BRIGID. … you must never say the word "scissoring" again…

RICHARD. I'm steering clear of this conversation…

ERIK. *(To Rich.)* Its *real* meaning is beautiful—it's old Irish custom to leave the door unbolted and a candle in the window for Mary on her way to Bethlehem.

AIMEE. Well, it's premature, but… in honor of you, Momo…

(A toast, struggling not to laugh.) May the Virgin and her Child lift all of your latches...

> *They all ad lib cheers, "Amen," "hear hear," etc... Erik lovingly disapproves of her joke, notices Momo's a bit dazed, her neck is not at a comfortable angle.*

ERIK. Okay, this isn't gonna [work]—she's gonna be dozing off soon, / lemme get her settled—

DEIRDRE. Want me to—

ERIK. —No I got it, I got it... keep eating guys...

> *Erik wheels Momo back to the couch, gets her settled there.*

DEIRDRE. Where's your family, Rich? They upset we stole you away?

RICHARD. Oh, they're good, thanks. My dad's in L.A. and my mom's on the Cape now.

DEIRDRE. What cape?

BRIGID. Cape Horn, Mom—you know he's from / Massachusetts—

AIMEE. Hey, hey... it's not a dumb / question...

BRIGID. Cape *Cod*, sorry... I'm sorry.

DEIRDRE. What's your mom do, Rich?

RICHARD. She's a therapist... / she works from home... yeah...

DEIRDRE. Oh wow, that's great... do you guys have any Thanksgiving traditions?

RICHARD. Uh, some, yeah, we usually start our morning off volunteering at this soup kitchen about thirty minutes from our house, so...

DEIRDRE. That's beautiful, I volunteer with the Bhutanese now, / every week they have—

BRIGID. Mom, we know.

RICHARD.   AIMEE. *(To Brigid.)*
No, I'm interested…   [Why are you being such a bitch?]

DEIRDRE. They uh, the Bhutanese, the level of poverty, guys, is just… [unimaginable…]

> *They eat. Erik returns to the table after getting Momo settled.*

ERIK. *(To Rich.)* You balancing a job with all your studies… or just racking up the college loans?

RICHARD. Ha, I've gone the loan route but I plan on paying them off as soon as possible…

BRIGID. His grandmother—he's getting a small trust when he turns forty—can I tell them?

RICHARD. You want to know if you can tell them *after* you tell them? / Seriously?

DEIRDRE.   AIMEE.
Like a trust fund?   Pass the… / yeah, thanks…

BRIGID. Sorry—babe, sorry, don't be embarrassed…

RICHARD.   BRIGID.
I'm *not* embarrassed—   —it's actually great—his
                                        grandmother didn't want him
                                        spoiled so he doesn't see any
                                        of the money until he's forty.

ERIK. *(Teasing.)* You haven't reached that milestone yet, Rich?

BRIGID.   RICHARD. *(Smiling.)*
Ha, ha…   No, not quite, I'm thirty-eight…

DEIRDRE. Having to wait until your forties is a—your grandma's a smart lady, it's like that—'member that email I forwarded you guys about Andrew Carnegie—is it *Car*negie or Car*neg*ie, / I never remember…

RICHARD.   ERIK.
Pretty sure Car*neg*ie is correct…   *Car*negie Hall, right?
oh, maybe, yeah…   *Car*negie Hall…

DEIRDRE. I forwarded it, Rich, 'cause it had this great answer to the question: "What makes Americans powerful and influential and wealthy?"

> *Small beat as they eat.*

AIMEE. Trust funds?

DEIRDRE. No… not trust funds, / smart-ass…

AIMEE. What—too soon? Too soon?…

BRIGID. Yes, too soon…

DEIRDRE. What makes a person powerful and influential and wealthy is *not* growing up with power and influence and wealth. That's what the email said, anyway… *(Caught off-guard by her emotions.)* … The gift of poverty is a… it's not a myth, / it's a real thing, it can be a blessing…

AIMEE. Whoa, Mom, are you okay?

DEIRDRE. Yeah I'm just happy to be with my girls, sorry…

> *They eat. Brigid mouths, "Get a grip…" to herself.*
> *Erik cracks open another beer.*

ERIK. One thing I learned, Rich—and the older I get I see this—it's that having too much money—it can be just as bad for you as, you know, *not* having enough, / you know? Gotta be careful…

BRIGID. *(Embarrassed.)* Dad, why're you—what are you talking about—

RICHARD. I think I know what you're saying—do you mean—

ERIK. I'm saying—Dee's bosses have more money than God and they're stingy with her on everything, bonuses, vacation days… Aimes gets fired 'cause she's sick—*my* grandma almost lost her life in a fire 'cause her bosses locked the doors to her factory to keep 'em from takin' breaks, coupla blocks from here, so—and this isn't some scientific notion or something—but, yeah, I do notice that rich people are usually pretty messed up.

BRIGID.	AIMEE.
[Oh God…]	That's an elegant thesis, Dad.

RICHARD. Well, no, no, it's a good point, I just don't think being messed up is *necessarily* linked to how much money is in your bank account.

BRIGID.	ERIK.
Of course…	Yeah, but it *can* shift your priorities in ways that aren't good.

RICHARD. We agree on that, yeah, but so can being poor. Right? / Just meaning—

BRIGID. Yes…

AIMEE. Everyone's right, guys…

RICHARD. —I actually agree with you, I'm just adding that… yes, wealth can ruin people but so can poverty.

DEIRDRE. Well I'd rather be ruined in a Four Seasons somewhere, on a beach, you know?… I'll take wealth for four hundred, Alex…

BRIGID.	AIMEE.
Mom, that doesn't even make sense…	Oh, Mom…

RICHARD. … I hear you, I'm just proud that my family went out of their way to ensure—you *do* get that I'm not able to touch my money until I'm forty, right?

ERIK. Uh-huh, but do *you* get how that sounds to a man my age?

RICHARD. No I hear you, I hear you… / I do…

BRIGID.	AIMEE.
We got the veggies from this	… pass the—thanks…
farmer's market on Essex…	

DEIRDRE. They're delicious…

BRIGID. We're gonna try and keep our fridge stocked with them, start juicing for breakfast.

AIMEE. Cool…

RICHARD. You guys liking any of the superfoods?

BRIGID. *(To Aimee.)* Rich made up a *list* that I emailed to these guys…

DEIRDRE. I even, I bought blueberries last week… they're not cheap.

ERIK. You also bought blueberry donuts.

DEIRDRE. Yeah, and you had three of them, so don't / act like you're better than me please.

ERIK. I did, no, I did.

AIMEE. Sadly, donuts are cheaper, too, huh?

DEIRDRE.	BRIGID.
Yeah.	Not cheaper when you consider
	how much heart disease costs once
	you're hospitalized.

    They eat.

ERIK. So what, uh, when forty comes along, what happens… do you just, do you retire?

AIMEE.	BRIGID.
Dad…	No, he's studying to become a social worker…

RICHARD. Yeah, the main reason I'm not done with school yet is, I've been / in and out—

BRIGID. He took time off—

RICHARD. —Yeah, because for a while / I was—

BRIGID. You don't have to tell them…

RICHARD. —It's fine—in my early thirties—I was depressed for a bit, so—I'm fine now, just took me a while to get up and running again, but… I've been better for years, it's why I'm comfortable talking about it…

ERIK. You take medicine for that?

BRIGID. Dad, that's rude / to ask—

ERIK.	RICHARD.
Sorry, hey, sorry, just… in our family we don't, uh, we don't have that kinda depression.	It's okay.

AIMEE. Yeah, no we just have a lot of stoic sadness.

They eat.

ERIK. *(To Rich.)* Well… I'm sorry, if—

RICHARD. [It's fine.]

ERIK. … Makes you wonder if—the kind of faith *we* grew up with… it's not perfect but you take for granted what a, a, a kinda natural anti-depressant it is…

AIMEE. No religion at the table—

DEIRDRE. Hey, my mouth is shut, you know / where I stand…

BRIGID. Mom… you brought a statue of the Virgin Mary into our house— / how is your mouth shut?

ERIK. Alright, okay… I didn't mean to get us… I was just saying it's funny you guys'll try—you put faith in, in juice-cleansing or / yoga but you won't try church—

BRIGID. I did *one* juice cleanse… *one*…

ERIK.	DEIRDRE.
—You eat chard to feel your best but you still—you said half your friends are in therapy, / *you* said that so I'm askin'—	My mouth is shut…

BRIGID. That's because—yeah, I was trying to get you to pay for *mine*—I still can't afford it—

ERIK. Well save some of the money you spend on organic juice and pay for it yourself—

BRIGID. Don't criticize me for caring about my mental health—

AIMEE. Okay…

ERIK. Well what about—Rich's mom is a therapist—why don't you get it from her?—

DEIRDRE.	BRIGID.
Erik…	Yeah, Dad, I'll get therapy from my mother-in-law, that's an awesome idea.

    Small beat.

DEIRDRE. She's not your mother-in-law unless you get married—

AIMEE. Mom… [don't…]

BRIGID. Looking for work every day, it's depressing—

ERIK. Well you've still got the will to eat superfoods—if you're so miserable why're you trying to live forever?

Aimee smiles involuntarily.

BRIGID. Last week—I shouldn't even tell you—

ERIK.
Tell us what?

BRIGID.
Babe, you don't have to—

Babe—

RICHARD.
I don't think you appreciate how hard she's been working… She's been bartending at two places while applying for every possible artist grant or residency you can think of… *(To Brigid.)* … tell them, you'll feel better…

ERIK.
Tell us what?

BRIGID.
He won't care…

RICHARD.
You'll feel better…

DEIRDRE.
Tell us…

ERIK. Of course I'll care.

RICHARD. Read it to him, you'll feel better.

Brigid gets out her phone, searches for something.

This one professor has been writing all of her recommendation letters for all these applications and—

BRIGID. Yeah 'cause there's only one that I felt close to at school, who actually knew who I was, so… I was gonna miss this one deadline so I called his office and… his assistant agreed to email the rec letter directly to me…

Brigid hands her iPhone to Erik, who reads the PDF of the letter on her phone.

AIMEE. What's it say?

BRIGID. ... at least now I know why I'm not even getting interviews for unpaid internships.

ERIK. *(Reading.)* What's the big deal?—he didn't praise you enough?

Pissed, Brigid grabs her phone.

BRIGID. Are you kidding me? *(Reading.)* "Brigid is a talented musician and composer; she served as a TA in my music theory class her senior year and many of the students noted how approachable and helpful she was to them in navigating the course. Initially, I must confess, I found Brigid's compositions almost willfully opposed to specificity and urgency. In her senior year, however, she showed marked improvement. And while her orchestral pieces still do not have the range or originality of her contemporaries, she always displays technical proficiency and great verve [What does that even mean?!]. Her hard work and positive attitude have made her an asset to the music department." *(Eyes watering.)* ... Why wouldn't he respect me enough to say he couldn't do it?

Richard comforts her.

ERIK. You can always work retail.

DEIRDRE.
Don't / tease her, babe—

AIMEE.
Dad—Bridge, he's a dick for writing this—

RICHARD.
It's not easy to bounce back from this kind of thing, Erik—

ERIK.
... Oh c'mon, hey, Rich don't treat me like—she knows I believe in her. *(To Brigid.)* —Are you so spoiled you can't see you're crying over something hard work can fix?—

BRIGID. Everyone whose opinion I value has read this—

ERIK. Your grandma grew up in a two-room cesspool and your tragedy is what—havin' to figure out how to get a new letter of recommendation? / Sorry if I—

BRIGID.
It takes *years* to build rela-
tionships with—

DEIRDRE.
She knows all this…

ERIK. —You're lucky to have a passion to pursue, if you don't care about it enough to push through this setback you should quit and do something else…

DEIRDRE.
Alright… we're sorry,
Bridge, that guy's a jerk…

AIMEE. *(To Erik.)*
Wow, what is up with you today?

> **Upstairs:** *The light near the staircase burns out. The only light upstairs comes from the crack in the bathroom door (which is mostly shut) and the indirect light being thrown by the LED lantern in the recesses of the upstairs space.*

BRIGID.
Shit, another bulb's out…

RICHARD.
Oh great…
Welcome to New York, guys…

DEIRDRE. It's just a light bulb… we'll live…

> *Brigid goes in search of a spare bulb. Erik follows her.*

ERIK. *(To Brigid, who is still angry with him.)* Hey, hey, I don't wanna see you bent outta shape over something you can fix. / The Blakes bounce back, that's what we do.

BRIGID. Thanks… uh-huh, yeah… thanks Dad, I don't really need a lecture now… Rich—why didn't we ask the landlord to replace all the lightbulbs before we moved in?

RICHARD. Because that's a crazy thing to ask for, babe, no one asks for that.

DEIRDRE. *(Stifling laughter.)*
Yeah, no one asks for that /
… and even if you did, it
wouldn't matter, 'cause…

ERIK.
Well, they're all probably on
their last legs…

AIMEE. What are you laughing at?

DEIRDRE. ... she's burning out the bulbs to get our attention...

BRIGID.	AIMEE.
What?	What—who is?

DEIRDRE. She-With-No-Face... / she strikes again!

ERIK.	AIMEE.
Now you got her started...	What's so funny? What?

BRIGID. Dad sees faceless women in his sleep...

DEIRDRE. *(Going upstairs, wobbly ghost wail.)* ... woooooooo...

RICHARD. Tough crowd, Erik...

AIMEE.	ERIK.
Where are you going, crazy lady?	You're tellin' me...

DEIRDRE. The bathroom... *(Using a flashlight.)* ... this is gonna be like spelunking just to go pee... woooooo...

> **Downstairs:** *Now they are all laughing, even Richard.*

> **Upstairs:** *Deirdre proceeds to the bathroom.*

AIMEE. Who is this headless person?

BRIGID. *Faceless,* she's got skin covering her eye sockets / and mouth—

AIMEE.	ERIK.
Ewwwww...	Alright, ha, ha...

> *Brigid, still miffed by Erik's tough love, gets up to go to the kitchen area.*

BRIGID. ... Yeah, and I hope she visits you tonight in your sleep and casts an evil spell / on you—

ERIK. Oh yeah, smart-ass?—

> *Erik stops Brigid and bear-hugs her, making her laugh involuntarily.*

BRIGID.
Stop! Dad! Oh *now* you wanna be compassionate?! Stop! The eyeless sorceress has all my support…

ERIK.
You don't know how good you have it…

RICHARD. Last week I dreamed I fell into an ice cream cone made of grass and became a baby.

BRIGID. Richard, / are you kidding me with the sharing…

RICHARD. What?—I can share it if I want / —I restarted my life…

BRIGID. You can, and I love you, but when you share dreams in front of my family I become a crazy / person—

AIMEE. Hey, why don't—alright, Lover-of-all, come on, come with me, let's get rid of some of this…

RICHARD. You want help?

AIMEE. No, you're good, you're good…

> *Aimee and Brigid exit into the kitchen. Aimee is half-heard saying, "C'mon Princess, step into my office…" as they ad-lib their way into the kitchen, carrying food dishes.*

RICHARD. I got to reboot my life, it was good…

ERIK. I dunno. Doing life twice sounds like the only thing worse than doing it once.

> *They drink. Audible-but-indecipherable conversation from Aimee and Brigid in the kitchen.*

RICHARD. The cone was made out of grass from my backyard…?

ERIK. *(Smiling.)* Out of / your backyard?…

RICHARD. … My backyard?… like it got twisted into an ice cream cone?… In my head it was so normal…

> *They drink. Audible-but-indecipherable conversation from Aimee and Brigid in the kitchen.*

ERIK. In mine there was this one other weird thing I… [remember…]

RICHARD. In your dream?

ERIK. *(Nodding.)* [Yeah]… I didn't bring it up with—
The girls already think I'm losing it, you know but—
the woman without a [face]…
she's trying to get me in this, like a tunnel?

RICHARD. Yeah? And what do you do?

ERIK. Uh… I don't move, I dunno…

> *Erik shrugs it off, not wanting it to seem like a big deal. More audible-but-indecipherable conversation and laughs from Brigid/Aimee in the kitchen.*

RICHARD. What's going on in there?

BRIGID. *(O.S.)* None of your business!

> *They drink.*

RICHARD. Tunnels are—in my class we got this list of primitive settings?—tunnels and caves, forests, the sea… Stuff so a part of us it's… you know, two hundred thousand years ago… someone might've… closed their eyes and… seen a similar kind of [image]…?

> *A mechanical RUMBLE sounds from behind the basement door.*

Trash compactor.

> *They drink. The RUMBLE stops.*

Get in it next time, the tunnel…

ERIK. *(Lighthearted.)* Thanks, / I'll try that…

RICHARD. I'm serious, get in it next time—
tunnels can just be,
stuff hidden from yourself?
so passing through one... [I dunno...] could be...
a favorable omen... you know?

ERIK. Is it a fortune-telling school you're at?

RICHARD. *(Smiling.)* No...

ERIK. —"a favorable omen"?—

RICHARD. ... No it is not...

ERIK. —You sure? You gonna bring out a crystal ball later?

> *Clank of pre-war pipes.*
> *The noise covers Deirdre opening the bathroom door.*
> *The girls return from the kitchen, laughing.*

RICHARD. *(Re: their laughing.)* What?

AIMEE. We're conferring about... Mom's latest email forward, /
oh man...

BRIGID. *(Laughing.)*	ERIK.
Did you get it, Dad?...	Hey, hey shhhh...

> **Upstairs:** *Deirdre stops in her tracks. We realize she can (most*
> *likely) hear their discussion.*

AIMEE. *(To Rich.)* Rich, the subject line was: "PLEASE READ
THIS" in all-caps, all-caps—so the email got flagged by my IT
department for being "potentially harmful"...

BRIGID. [Yeah,] which was kinda prophetic.

RICHARD. Why—what did it say?

BRIGID. She forwarded a *Scientific American* article about how...
nothing's solid; when you're touching a table, you're really feeling

its molecules bouncing against—*we're* not even solid, we're, what...
electrons / pushing back against everything...?

AIMEE. Electrons, yeah... it also had vague religious overtones,
there was a poem at the bottom in about ten fonts about how we
already *are* a part of everything, how—

ERIK. Hey don't make fun of your mom, / no, I'm serious—

BRIGID.	AIMEE.
We're making fun	Dad, come on, it was
of the email...	a *little* crazy—

AIMEE. —it was like: "Happy Tuesday, oh and just FYI: at the
subatomic level, everything is chaotic and unstable... love, Mom."

ERIK. You have to start writing her back, okay? / I mean it... even
to stuff like that...

AIMEE. You're right.

BRIGID. I know, I will...

> **Upstairs***: So they won't know she's been listening, Deirdre
> walks to the bathroom door and shuts it again.*

> **Downstairs***, they acknowledge the door shutting.*

ERIK. ... Rich, I hope you don't think the Blakes're [insensitive]...
we're better than that, / we're drinking a bit too much here...

RICHARD.	BRIGID.
No, no way... and hey... no... If my	He doesn't think
family's meals *are* any calmer it's only	that...
because, the joke in my family is that our	
holidays are all sponsored by Klonopin,	
so /... or so the joke goes...	

BRIGID.	ERIK.
Richard...	What's that?

| AIMEE. | RICHARD. |
| Just, it's medicine… | … sorry, [bad joke…] |

Deirdre is now descending the staircase. Momo moans a bit in her sleep.

MOMO. *(Mumbled.)* … you can never come black… / you can never come back you can never come back you can never come back you can never come back…

DEIRDRE. *(To Erik, checking on Momo.)* I got it, stay down…

Laundry room noise sounds from behind the basement door.

BRIGID. That's the laundry room. That'll die down…

DEIRDRE. What kind of people would do laundry on Thanksgiving?

BRIGID. Mom, Chinese people.

The laundry room noise dies down.

Having all this space makes it worth it… putting up with the noise.

AIMEE. *(Clearing plates.)* … You done, Mom?

ERIK.	DEIRDRE. *(Tending to*
The, uh… I should say the other	*Momo.)*
other thing I was… wanted to,	Yeah, I'm full…
uh… whoa… man, I haven't had	
that much to drink but my thought	
train just got all—	

AIMEE. Your "thought train"? / Yeah I'd say your thought train just got derailed…

BRIGID. Stop drinking, then…

AIMEE. … I'm gonna have to call you a car, unless…

DEIRDRE.
… Erik…

ERIK.
No I'll stop drinking,
I'm done…

BRIGID. But unless you camp out here for a few more hours—

ERIK.
Don't worry about me, I'm fine—
I was trying to remember the pig
smash, that's what I'm— / we're
forgetting about our pig smash…

AIMEE.
You're too—Dad, grow up.
I'm calling you a car…

DEIRDRE.
Okay, but… not sure we [should
until]—

BRIGID.
Oh good idea, let's do it
now…

RICHARD. Someone needs to explain the rules…

BRIGID. It's very simple…

AIMEE. Mom, get over here, we're pig-smashing.

BRIGID. … We each pass it around, say what we're thankful for,
then we smash the pig…

AIMEE. And then we each eat a piece of the peppermint for good
luck.

RICHARD. That is the weirdest tradition—

DEIRDRE. Please, *that's* the weirdest…? Wait until you spend a
Christmas with us…

ERIK. She's threatening to invite all the Bhutanese in Scranton
over for caroling.

DEIRDRE. Oh that's not a threat, honey, that's happening.

BRIGID. Here we go, why don't you start, babe.

RICHARD. Ah, now I'm nervous. Okay, uh… this year I'm most thankful for falling in love with Brigid… And for… getting a new family in the process. *("Awwww"s from everyone.)* Now I… [smash the pig?…]

He takes the tiny mallet and smashes the pig.

BRIGID. *(With love.)* That was a terrible smash… / do it harder…

RICHARD. Well I don't know… you made me go first!

BRIGID.   AIMEE.
Okay, Dad you go next…   Rich, it was a fine smash…

ERIK. Okay, well… I already gave one speech so lemme just say… I'm thankful for having your unconditional love and support. Hope there's nothing any of us could ever do to… change that… what we've got right here, 'cause this is what matters… this family…

He smashes the pig, passes the mallet to Deirdre.

DEIRDRE. Alright, well I'm with your dad and—it may sound cliché, but I'm thankful for the both of you…

Deirdre smashes the pig. She then hands the mallet to Brigid.

BRIGID. Okay… I'll state the obvious, there will never be a year I'm not thankful that the observation deck didn't open until 9:30… so… And I'm grateful Momo's with us… oh— *(To Erik.)* A wise, old, haggard drunk man once told me that pursuing your passion is a gift—so I'm grateful for that reminder… even if I end up pursuing it while managing an H&M, / I'm lucky… No I'm actually being serious about that, I am…

AIMEE.   DEIRDRE.
Ohhh so soon, so soon…   See what you've done?

BRIGID. *(She's about to smash, then—)* And while everyone's [all here]—if anything were to ever happen to me, like an accident or whatever—and it won't, but: I'd want to be cremated—I know it's weird to talk about but you guys'd do open-casket so… I've been trying to find a way to bring it up that isn't morbid or weird.

AIMEE. Well you didn't find it, Bridge.

> *Erik and Aimee are now laughing. Eventually Richard joins them.*

DEIRDRE.
Are you serious? You're crazy.

BRIGID.
Oh come on—I *am* seri—…
You're crazy… / no one in this
family can handle honesty…

ERIK. You are a piece of work… God bless you, you are…

AIMEE. No you're right, Bridge, dinner is the perfect place to discuss what we should do with your dead body… / thank you…

BRIGID. I hate you all.

AIMEE. … Pass me that pig. *(Beat.)* Alright. So. In a year where— I lost my job, my girlfriend, and I'm bleeding internally… really a banner year… I'm thankful for what's *right*, okay? I *love* that in times like this I have a home base, a family I can always come home to. Thanks for giving us that.

BRIGID. You always have to win.

RICHARD. Yeah, she really *cremated* you.

> *Richard's joke is so lame it makes everyone laugh.*

BRIGID. Wow just when you can't get / less funny…

DEIRDRE. *(Laughing.)* She cremated you! She really cremated you… oh man…

> *They recover.*

ERIK. How about for Momo—should we read Momo's email?

BRIGID.
Dad, no, it makes us cry—

AIMEE.
Oh God…
… get out the Kleenex…

ERIK. This might be our last Thanksgiving together, can we please give her a voice…?

BRIGID.   AIMEE.
Of course…   Yeah, has he heard this?

RICHARD. I heard about it, but not the actual…

ERIK. She wrote this before she got really sick, Rich… an email to these girls, what four years ago?

Erik finds the message on his phone.

DEIRDRE. Here, give it to me, you're gonna end up asking me to finish…

Erik hands her his phone.

"Dear Aimee and Brigid, I was clumsy around you both today and felt confused. I couldn't remember your names and felt bad about that. It's strange slowly becoming someone I don't know. But while I *am* still here, I want to say: Don't worry about me once I drift off for good. I'm not scared. If anything, I wish I could've known that most of the stuff I *did* spend my life worrying about wasn't so bad. Maybe it's because this disease has me forgetting the worst stuff, but right now I'm feeling nothing about this life was worth getting so worked up about. Not even dancing at weddings."

The Blakes smile. They have inside understanding of this remark.

"Dancing at weddings always scared the crap out of me, but now it doesn't seem like such a big deal. This is taking me forever to type. Consider this my fond farewell. *Erin go bragh.* Dance more than I did. Drink less than I did. Go to church. Be good to everyone you love. I love you more than you'll ever know."

They recover, some quiet tears of appreciation. They pass around the smashed pieces of peppermint; they each take a bite, one at a time.

RICHARD. I'm buying a pig for my family.

Richard starts to clear plates, goes to the kitchen.

BRIGID. *(To Erik.)* He wants you to like him.

DEIRDRE.   AIMEE.
We love him…   We do…

ERIK. Yeah, just look out for each other, okay?, that's what counts…

> *Erik goes to the kitchen for a beer.*

DEIRDRE. Amen… in sickness and health /… for richer for poorer…

AIMEE. Tell that to Carol… *(To Erik.)* Hey if you're having another beer, fine, but I'm calling a car for you guys…

BRIGID.   DEIRDRE.
Thanks for drinking responsibly, Dad.   Erik…

ERIK. I'm forgetting I'm not home, I'm sorry… I'm sorry…

AIMEE. I don't mind using my work account now that I'm on my way out—

ERIK.   DEIRDRE.
No way, that's gonna cost   No way, no, I'll drive,
a fortune…   I've been drinkin' water…

AIMEE.   BRIGID.
This is on me, it's not up   Mom for like the last
for discussion—   ten minutes.

ERIK. No way, what'd we do about our car?

> *Aimee is already on her way upstairs.*

AIMEE. I'm calling a car, / end of discussion.

BRIGID. Rich can drive it in tomorrow or—bus it into the city and help us paint this weekend, okay? We'll put you to work, just / take the car…

ERIK. Yeah, just, I'm not used to driving on Thanksgiving, Rich—

RICHARD. No worries—Bridge, should we repark the car? I think it's street cleaning in the morning but... we'll figure it out...

> *Brigid mouths "Thank you, I love you" into Richard's ear. They kiss. Their affection for each other triggers something in Erik—embarrassment that Richard needed to take care of him? Nostalgia for his own early romance with Deirdre?*
> *The stage picture should subtly highlight Brigid and Rich's flawed-but-alive connection and a gulf between Erik and Deirdre. Erik decides to go upstairs.*

> **Upstairs**: *Aimee has dialed her cell...*

AIMEE. Hi I need a car... Yeah, just charge it to my account... right, it's—Zip is 18433... Scott Township, Pennsylania... no case number, take it out of my personal... yeah, exactly... Uh, three— but one of them is in a wheelchair— *(To Erik, who has arrived upstairs.)* Do you guys need a van for Momo...?—

ERIK.
Here, give it here... *(Mouths "go downstairs" to Aimee. On the phone:)* ... Hi, yeah three but... we don't need a van it'll fit in the trunk, it folds... uh-huh... a lot cheaper or—?... then a van's good then that's fine... uh-huh... yeah, uh-huh... *(Wandering farther back.)* Can I use a credit card for... Yeah, but I'm gonna be paying her back so how much is— [wow, that's a lot...] yeah...

> **Downstairs**:
> *Richard and Brigid continue bussing dishes; they set out a dessert tray and some ice cream and spoons.*
>
> *Deirdre—unseen by anyone—is silently overcome with emotion, covers her face to stifle sobs.*

> *Erik wanders away from Aimee to finish the call with some privacy. He finishes the call—including giving the car company his cell phone number—his back to us; he's half-audible, not decipherable. Aimee rolls her eyes at Erik ordering the van; she goes downstairs. Deirdre recovers from her crying spell when she hears Aimee coming downstairs.*

RICHARD. Dessert is on the way...

AIMEE. Thank you... So's a car...

DEIRDRE. Oh man, I can't believe there's more food...

> *Aimee helps bus some more dirty dishes to the kitchen. Sensing Deirdre's a bit distressed:*

AIMEE. Mom, don't worry about it, it saves me a cab ride—I can hitch a ride with you guys to Penn Station...

ERIK. *(Descending the stairs.)* Okay, they'll come at six... but we can change the time if you want...

AIMEE.	DEIRDRE.
Okay, I can make a 7:05 train.	Sounds good...

DEIRDRE. Thanks, Aimee, I'm embarrassed we had to do this—

AIMEE. Hey, first time for everything, right?

> *Erik hands Aimee her phone. Aimee returns to the kitchen to help.*

DEIRDRE. *(To Erik.)* Are you too drunk to thank your daughter?

> *Brigid is upstage, talking to Aimee from the kitchen. They do not hear Erik and Deirdre's conversation.*

BRIGID. This is all from a local bakery...

DEIRDRE. *(More pointed.)* Hey, are you too drunk to thank your daughter?

> *This pisses Erik off, but he ignores Deirdre.*
> *Richard joins the table.*

RICHARD. So what we've got is—this is rugelach, vanilla cupcakes, a chocolate croissant...

DEIRDRE. Wow... well today I officially fell off the Weight Watchers wagon, so... Man, these all look good... I'll have, uh... I'll have—

ERIK. Give her the one with all the frosting, that's the one she wants.

> *Beat. That was the one Deirdre wanted, but now she's too stung.*

DEIRDRE. I'll have, the, uh… I'll, uh… / I'm gonna…

RICHARD. Which one can I get you?

DEIRDRE. Just gonna /… [sit here for a minute…]

MOMO. *(Waking, barely audible, mumbled.)* … nairywheres do we blag werstrus, doll sezzer / big sussten back… sezz it whairidoll… er hairin sildern fernal garn ackening ery or loddinsezz…

DEIRDRE.	BRIGID.
… I'm gonna take her to the bathroom, yeah Erik?… / okay?…	You okay, Momes?…

BRIGID.	ERIK.
I can help you—	Yeah…

DEIRDRE. No I'm good.

ERIK. *(To Richard.)* Would you help her get Momo settled upstairs, / I don't want her lifting her by herself…

RICHARD. Sure…

BRIGID. Dad, I said *I'd* help…

ERIK. No, stay here, will you? / Stay here…

> *Deirdre assists Momo into her wheelchair as Aimee returns from the kitchen.*

BRIGID. Why?

ERIK. I wanna talk to you guys about how…

AIMEE. What?

ERIK. ... We might be movin' soon if, uh—

DEIRDRE. *(Wheeling Momo out.)* There we go, Mom...

AIMEE. But I thought—the sewers won't be in yet...

Deirdre continues to roll Momo towards the basement door.

DEIRDRE.
Yeah, tell 'em about
the sewers.

MOMO. *(Mumbling unintelli-gibly until she exits.)* ... wheres'll her annear... do you go hole in a wheres do you go hole in a wheres do go hole in a where to go hole in a wheres... where do we go hole in a...

AIMEE.
What's going on?

BRIGID.
... Mom... [what's wrong?...]

ERIK.
Nothing, nothing stay here
okay?—everyone's okay...
(To Richard.) Would you let
them in upstairs?

DEIRDRE. *(To Brigid.)*
I'm okay, stay here...

Deirdre and Momo exit.

RICHARD. Sure...

BRIGID.
Dad. What's wrong?

Upstairs:
Richard goes upstairs, opens the upstairs door and waits offstage in the hallway for Momo and Deirdre to get off the elevator.

ERIK.
Nothing, everyone's okay,
alright?...

AIMEE.
Are you sick?

ERIK. No no, relax, no one's sick, we're good, just, we sold the lake property, okay? / To help with—

AIMEE.	BRIGID.
Okay...	What... when...?

ERIK. [Not important]... St. Paul's let me go, okay, so we've had to / tighten our belts and we're figuring out—

BRIGID. Why would they let you go?

ERIK. —That's not [important]—I'm not getting my pension now, they could fire me before it kicked in, alright / so now—

AIMEE. They can take away / your pension—?

ERIK. It's [complicated]—they're a private school so / they can do whatever—

AIMEE. But—why did they fire you?

ERIK. It's [complicated]—they have this morality code, okay?, / St. Paul's makes—

AIMEE. Okay...

ERIK. —you sign it / and if you—

BRIGID. Why would a morality code—were you, like, selling drugs on the playground?

ERIK. There was an incident and... alright?, so / they could—

BRIGID. What kind of—

ERIK. They could fire me... because of this incident, it's—

AIMEE. What are you talking about?

ERIK. I cheated on your mom, with, uh, a teacher from school and... we're okay but, I realize this is a lot to just [unload]... You guys okay?—

AIMEE.	BRIGID.
[Uh, not really...]	Just... [keep going...]

ERIK. —We worked through it, okay?, / we met with Father Quinn and...

AIMEE. Okay...

ERIK. ... We're good, but people talk and we don't want you hearing from other people, okay? / We'd rather you hear it from us, okay?...

AIMEE. Okay, so... okay, so you guys... you just want us to... just... to know?...

ERIK. Yeah, and I'm already at a Walmart in Danville / just to keep money coming in—

AIMEE. God, Dad... for how long?—

BRIGID. Why the one in Danville?

ERIK. I don't want kids from school seeing me there. Something full-time should open up this spring, so... / the trick's been...

AIMEE. ... so...

ERIK. ... the cost of taking care of Momo's been a surprise, / you wouldn't even believe how much the [medical stuff costs]—

BRIGID.	AIMEE.
Are you guys...	... okay...
	So you're behind?
	How much are you behind?
	ERIK.
Can Mom not retire now?—	I don't want you [worrying about]—

AIMEE. Would I be able to help out?… or—is it too much for me to even—

ERIK. I think—you've lost your job / and'll have your own medical stuff to [worry about]—

AIMEE. Okay, I know, I know but I still want to know how deep a hole you're in.

> *Being buzzed almost makes things worse for Aimee and Brigid.*

> **Upstairs**: *Richard now holds the door open; Deirdre wheels Momo inside. She doesn't get far before she hears the discussion downstairs; it stops her from taking Momo to the bathroom. Instead, Deirdre goes to the top of the stairs to listen. Richard instinctively goes to Momo, waits with her…*

ERIK. The plan is to sell the house and rent an apartment, we don't need space / anymore…

BRIGID. Are there even apartments in Scranton? / Who lives in—

ERIK.	AIMEE.
Hey, getting a place on one level will be good, Mom won't be climbing stairs—	Of course there are—

AIMEE. It doesn't sound good, Dad / —it sounds like you're in a deep hole—

ERIK. I'm working it out, Aimee—

AIMEE. Do you have *anything* saved? *Dad*, do you have any / savings?—

ERIK. We don't *have* savings, Aimee / *we've been stretched*—

AIMEE. —Okay, okay *well you're telling us this when you're drunk* / so sorry if I'm getting frustrated…

ERIK. —Well we haven't had savings for years.

103

BRIGID. Have you asked Uncle John to help?

AIMEE. He lives in a trailer, / you think—

BRIGID. That doesn't mean he has no money—

AIMEE. That's *exactly* what it means, / grow up... [fucking baby...]

BRIGID.
Relax, I'm just... [I'm shocked,
I don't know what I'm saying...]
Sorry I'm not grown up like you
and make a ton of money—

ERIK.
Don't get upset with
her, hey this is on me—

AIMEE. Right, you've got no choice but to collect unemployment / while you try to—it's not unfair for you to get some marketable skills—

ERIK.
Hey easy, cut it out. Stop it, both
of you, stop this is on me and—
(Recognizing Brigid's distress.) —hey
I'm working it out, / I love your
mom, we're good...

BRIGID.
That's not fair—I can't get
a break if I'm working
full-time...

> *Brigid isn't sure what to do; something's fallen apart for her, thoughts spinning...*

> **Upstairs**: *Deirdre has decided to go downstairs; she begins her descent...*

BRIGID. No, I'm glad you're working it out but—you're *good* but you're not sleeping and Mom's still eating her feelings, / it's freaking me out—

AIMEE. *(Re: Deirdre at the top of the stairs.)* Brigid.

> *Brigid turns, sees Deirdre at the top of the staircase. She heads upstairs to apologize.*

BRIGID. Mom... / I didn't mean it...

ERIK. Stay here…

Aimee goes after Brigid.

Would you stay down here, please? Brigid!

AIMEE.	DEIRDRE.
Dad give her some space, okay, we're doing our best—	Go talk to your father, please, / I *know* you think somethin's wrong with me, it's not a newsflash.

BRIGID. Mom—I will, but—I don't [think that]—I think something's wrong with *everyone*—please don't act like a martyr / when I'm trying to apologize… You think *I'm* wrong to not wanna get married in a church so—

AIMEE. *(To Brigid.)*	MOMO. *(Barely audible.)*
Hey, hey, you're sorry, don't yell, at her okay /… just chill out?	Nevery blacken where you come back do we go do we wheren blezzick… blacken where you come back do we go do…

ERIK. Can you guys come down and talk to me please!

THUD.

BRIGID. *(To Richard.)* Can you go up and tell that lady how loud she's being?

ERIK.	RICHARD.
Brigid!	I will, just relax.

THUD.

AIMEE. Dad, / please shuttup…

BRIGID.	MOMO. *(Mumbled.)*
I'll do it myself… / I need a breather—	Nevery blacken where you come back do we go do we wheren blezzick…

Momo's growing agitation captures Aimee's attention. Deirdre is massaging Momo's hand, perhaps for herself as much as for Momo.

RICHARD. *(To Brigid.)*
Hey, hey hey no, no—
Let's go for a walk, okay?—

AIMEE. *(Re: Momo, to Deirdre.)*
… Is she okay?

Erik arrives at the top of the stairs.

ERIK. Brigid, please come talk to me.

BRIGID. *(To Erik.)* I'm gonna ask that woman to stop banging her fucking feet.

Brigid exits. This is worse than if she yelled at Erik. Richard stops Erik from following her.

RICHARD.
Hey, let me…

MOMO.
… nevery where do we go back do we never go hole you bitch / … nevery hole backenser he did thisserwe go black, go black…

Deirdre walks to the staircase.

DEIRDRE. I've gotta… [go get some water downstairs…] I can't hear her now…

ERIK.
Yeah, I got this…
(To Aimee.) Go with her?
She's okay, just give us some room… go with Mom, okay?
Go with Mom.

MOMO.
… nevery where do we go back do we never go hole you bitch… nevery black hole you do we you did this do we back…
(Fixed on Erik.) Go hole. Go hole! Go hole! / Ohhhhhh God they're everywhere! They're comin' to you you bitch what's wrong with you…

Aimee has never seen Momo like this. Aimee heads downstairs to look after Deirdre. Erik tends to Momo.

DEIRDRE. *(Descending the stairs, barely intelligible.)*
… what's wrong with me…

ERIK. *(To Momo.)*
Hey, hey… shhhh… shhhh…

Momo is having her first real fit of the day. It's pretty terrifying. Erik has seen it before, but it's still hard for him. It's like she's possessed.

ERIK.
Okay, okay, okay...
we'll go for a walk... okay...
shhhhhh... you're okay...
shhhh... shhhhhh... you're
okay... shhhhh... there we
go... there we go, shhhhh...
shhhhh... that's good, you're
okay... shhhhh...

MOMO.
... Go home to fuck you *you bitch!*... Aaaaawwwwhhhh... where do you go hole! They're comin to *what's wrong with you* did this... aaaawwwwhhhh... where do go hole in a wheres... *(Tapering to barely audible.)*
... where do go hole in a wheres do go hole in a wheres do go hole in a where do go hole in a wheres...

Upstairs: *Erik wheels Momo around like she's a baby, calming her. Her screams subside. During the following scene, Erik stays with her, maybe massaging/holding her hand... Is he comforting her or is she giving him comfort?*

Downstairs: *Deirdre sits on the couch, takes a glass of water from Aimee. Long beat.*

DEIRDRE. If I ever get like that... I don't ever want you guys to have to...

Beat.

AIMEE. Mom... I'm sorry.

Beat.

DEIRDRE. I'm sorry you're sick.

Beat.

(This has been on her mind...) That email about us being electrons wasn't *religious*—it was from a *science* website...

Beat.

... I drank too much. I gotta use the [bathroom]...

Deirdre starts up the staircase.

AIMEE. Mom—sorry, it smells really bad in there.

DEIRDRE. *(Not looking back, half to herself.)* Shoulda got Brigid that candle.

> **Upstairs**: *Deirdre passes Erik and Momo on her way to the bathroom.*

ERIK. Hey, sorry this was… [a total fucking nightmare…]

> *Erik goes to embrace Deirdre.*

DEIRDRE.	ERIK.
No, no, no… I don't feel good.	I love you.
(Re: Momo.) Lemme get her to the	
bathroom before we go…	
C'mon, Mom… there you go…	

> *Deirdre helps Momo into the bathroom as Aimee ascends the stairs and proceeds to put on her coat.*

AIMEE. I'm gonna go for a walk around the block…

ERIK. Are you okay? Hey are you—

AIMEE. Yeah, I want some air, Dad.

> *Erik nods. Aimee ignores him as she puts her coat on. Erik searches for something to bridge the gap, to stop her from going.*

ERIK. I've been losing sleep trying to—I was saying to Father Quinn in how… / just *thinking* about losing you guys gets me thinking about…

AIMEE. What're you [saying?]…

ERIK. … When you were gone, when—

AIMEE. What're you [saying?]…

ERIK. —this fireman was holding a body with your same suit on?…

AIMEE. Dad...

ERIK. ... but with a coata ash melted onto her?, like she got turned into a statue like...

AIMEE. Dad...

> *Aimee aches for her father and wants to stay, but she needs to take care of herself.*

ERIK. ... there was gray in her eyes and mouth even, it was... like her whole...

> *A discovery.*

[... face was gone...]

> *Aimee has already moved to leave, she doesn't register Erik's discovery.*

AIMEE. The car company will call when they're ready, leave your phone by the window so it'll ring.

> *Aimee exits.*
>
> *Erik is alone for a few beats, lost, processing his discovery.*
>
> *Toilet flush brings him back to reality.*
>
> *He takes out his phone per Aimee's instructions and places it on the windowsill when—*
>
> *He notices a shadow move in the alley—what was it?*
>
> *He gets the LED lantern from the other room and walks back to the window to get a better look, but it's so dark outside the glass mostly reflects his image. He stares for a few beats.*
>
> ***Downstairs**: A few pots and pans hanging on the edge of the drying rack (just visible in the kitchen alley) fall and CRASH to the floor.*

ERIK. *(Calling down.)* Brigid...?

> *No answer. Erik descends the spiral staircase...*

Downstairs:
Erik arrives downstairs, where it's brighter. Erik turns the lantern off, places it on the counter. He begins to pick up the pots and pans...

Upstairs:
Deirdre and Momo exit the bathroom. The main upstairs door opens, revealing Aimee. She holds the door open, allowing light to spill into the upstairs rooms.

AIMEE. Guys, the car's out front...

DEIRDRE. Alright, get her coat, will you?...

AIMEE. *(Looking for Erik.)* Is Dad...?

DEIRDRE. [I dunno...]

AIMEE. *(Calling down.)* ... Dad!

ERIK. *(Calling up.)* I heard you...

> *Aimee helps Deirdre get Momo into her coat and back into the wheelchair.*

DEIRDRE. Where's Brigid?

AIMEE. With Rich...

> *Deirdre looks to Aimee for more information as Aimee helps Momo into her coat.*

... She's embarrassed, she's... [I don't even wanna get into it.] *(Calling down.)* ... Dad!...

ERIK. *(Calling up.)* Yeah, coming...

> *Aimee wheels Momo out of the apartment, exiting with Momo's barely discernable mumbling trailing...*
> *Deirdre goes to exit, but stops, remembering something.*

110

DEIRDRE. *(To Erik, calling down.)* Hey, can you grab Mom's blanket and the pan we brought?

ERIK. Uh-huh.

Downstairs:	**Upstairs:**
Erik goes back to picking up the pots and pans that fell.	*Deirdre, alone.*
	She takes one last look around, gets an idea: she removes the Virgin Mary statue from her purse and places it in the windowsill. She exits.
Having cleaned up the pots and pans, Erik searches for the specific pan they brought; finding it, he exits the kitchen and places the pan on the table—	

Erik searches for the blanket. He finds the blanket near the couch. He folds it.

All of the downstairs lights flicker out.

Complete darkness.

ERIK. Shit.

*Erik puts the blanket down; he searches for the lantern on the counter, knocking over chairs at the table as he stumbles past...
then—*

Upstairs:	
In complete darkness, the phone vibrates and lights up in the upstairs windowsill; the phone vibrates.	
vibrates.	
vibrates.	
vibrates.	**Downstairs:**
	—Erik finally finds the lantern, turns
vibrates.	*it on. LED lantern in hand, he flips*

111

all the fuse box switches to no avail.

ERIK. [Was that the phone?]

He flips the fuse box switches again, then—LED lantern in hand—goes up the staircase to answer the phone.

vibrates.

Then stops. Then—

vibrates.

vibrates.

vibrates.

vibrates.

Erik arrives at the windowsill, picks up the phone.

ERIK. Hello?... hello—

The RUMBLE of the trash compactor strikes up again outside the basement door.

In the darkness, it sounds louder than before, more disturbing.

… Erik pockets his phone, follows the noise back downstairs.

The RUMBLE continues.

Erik heads down the hallway towards the origin of the noise—pushes through his anxiety, opens the basement door; fluorescent light from the hallway spills in—

The rumble of the trash compactor is now even louder but more familiar, more like a loud trash compactor.

The trash compactor completes its cycle.

Silence.

Erik comes back inside but the spring-hinged door doesn't stay open, plunging the place into darkness as it closes. Erik goes to get a chair to prop it open when—

A THUD from above the staircase startles him; he drops the lantern...

Sounds of Erik's heavy breathing, Erik groping for a chair, Erik dragging it to the main downstairs door…

Suddenly fluorescent hallway light spills into the space via the basement door.

Erik is propping it open with a chair. The downstairs is now brighter.

He picks up the dropped lantern from the floor, which has remained on, holds it up towards the direction of the stairs…

Then, from the depths of the basement hallway, a new sound.

… click-clack, click-clack, click-clack…

Erik backs away from the hallway entrance.

… click-clack, click-clack, click-clack…

Erik's breath shortens.

… click-clack, click-clack, click-clack…

Erik's heart pounds, he looks towards the door.

… click-CLACK, click-CLACK, click-CLACK…

In a breath, an elderly Chinese woman passes the basement door on her way down the hall, wheeling her laundry in a cheap metal cart with a busted wheel.

The sounds slowly disappears as she rolls the cart down the hall… click-clack, click-clack, click-clack… click-clack, click-clack, click-clack…

This perfectly ordinary event leaves Erik feeling overwhelmed; it triggers a few ugly sobs.

Erik's face is visible via the light of the lantern.

He is quietly terrified, mumbling the Hail Mary.

Is he recovering from a panic attack?

ERIK. [What's happening to me?... What's wrong with me? This cannot be happening to me... oh God, how could I have gotten that worked up?]

> *Downstairs: Erik can't quite move yet; he clutches a support beam or sits in a chair, taking steady breaths, trying to recover.*
>
> *Alone, Erik collects himself, still unsure of what just transpired. He goes into the kitchen and splashes some water on his face.*
>
> *Rattled, the event's released something for him—a strange weight's been lifted off his chest.*
>
> *He takes deep breaths, trying to ground himself.*
>
> *This should all last at least fifteen seconds.*
>
> *Upstairs: Brigid enters into the dark apartment, her figure backlit by light from the upstairs hallway.*

BRIGID. *(Calling down.)* Dad... the driver's gonna have to keep circling the block. Dad...?

ERIK. Yeah, no here I come...

> **Upstairs:**
> *Brigid searches for something more to say.*
> *She goes to leave.*
> *She stops in the doorway.*
> *Beat.*
>
> *She comes back in again, still searching for something to say.*

> **Downstairs:**
> *Erik finds the pan they brought.*
>
> *He goes to get the blanket...*

BRIGID. *(Calling down.)* It's a van for some reason, so... I can ride with you guys to Penn Station... I'll get out with Aimee there, take the subway back... it's not far.

ERIK. Thanks.

> *Upstairs: Brigid exits.*
>
> *Downstairs: Erik is still recovering...*

114

He picks up Momo's blanket.

Arms full, he realizes he's left the LED lantern lit on the table.

He puts his belongings down; turns the lantern off, darkening the basement.

This greatly sharpens the shaft of fluorescent hallway light pouring through the propped-open door.

It has a tunnel-like quality.

Erik picks up his belongings again, turns towards the door and notices the shaft of light.

He steps into it.

He considers it for a moment.

He takes a deep breath.

He walks towards the door.

With no remaining natural or electric light, the apartment's architecture seems to have vanished…

… even the indirect moonlight from the upstairs window is gone…

… the only defined shape comes from the lighted doorway.

Erik exits into the hallway and out of sight.

A very long beat.

Another very long beat.

Another very long beat.

The propped-open door begins to slowly close entirely on its own; the weight of the chair can no longer hold it open.

The door clicks shut, rendering the space a deep, true black.

End of Play

NOTES
(Use this space to make notes for your production)

NOTES

(Use this space to make notes for your production)

NOTES
(Use this space to make notes for your production)